HIS MAJESTY, QUEEN HATSHEPSUT

HIS MAJESTY, QUEEN HATSHEPSUT

DOROTHY SHARP CARTER

Illustrated by Michele Chessare

J. B. LIPPINCOTT   NEW YORK

For Jan and Jack

Thanks are due to the following for permission to reprint the copyrighted materials listed below:

Charles Scribner's Sons, for two quotations from *Development of Religion and Thought in Ancient Egypt* by James Henry Breasted. Copyright 1912 Charles Scribner's Sons; copyright renewed 1940 Charles Breasted. Reprinted with the permission of Charles Scribner's Sons.

Macmillan Publishing Company for three quotations from *Ancient Records of Egypt*, Volume II, by J. H. Breasted as quoted in *Lady of the Two Lands* by Leonard Cottrell. Reprinted with permission of Macmillan Publishing Company. Copyright © 1967 by Leonard Cottrell; and Bell & Hyman Limited, for the above-mentioned material as quoted in *Queen of the Pharaohs* by Leonard Cottrell.

Library of Congress Cataloging-in-Publication Data
Carter, Dorothy Sharp.
His majesty, Queen Hatshepsut.

Summary: A fictionalized account of the life of
Hatshepsut, a queen in ancient Egypt who declared
herself pharaoh and ruled as such for more than twenty
years.
   1. Hatshepsut, Queen of Egypt—Juvenile fiction.
[1. Hatshepsut, Queen of Egypt—Fiction. 2. Egypt—
Civilization—To 332 B.C.—Fiction. 3. Kings, queens,
rulers etc.—Fiction] I. Title.
PZ7.C2434Hi 1987   [Fic]   85-45855
ISBN 0-397-32178-3
ISBN 0-397-32179-1 (lib. bdg.)

CONTENTS

PROLOGUE

The history of Egypt, beginning about 3500 B.C., was characterized by long spans of stability broken by intervals of anarchy. After one such chaotic period Upper and Lower Egypt were again united into one nation by the warriors Kamose and his brother Ahmose. On becoming pharaoh of Egypt, Ahmose inaugurated the eighteenth dynasty, which then continued with his son Amenhotep, followed by Thutmose I, at which point my story begins.

No firm dates have been established for Hatshepsut. One source, the *Encyclopedia Britannica*, gives for her reign the years 1503–1482 B.C. It was the custom in Ancient Egypt for each king to start a new cycle of dating with his own period of rule; there was no historical continuity in their system. Within Hatshepsut's own time span I have taken liberties with some dates for the sake of a more coherent story.

With regard to place names I have used mainly the ancient name rather than the modern. Thus for Thebes I use No-Amon or the City, and for Memphis the early name of Hikuptah; Egypt is referred to as Upper and Lower Egypt, the Black Land, or the Two Lands (even after unification it was so called); Hatshepsut's mortuary temple at West-of-the-City is *zesru zeser*; Karnak is known as Ipet-Isut and Luxor as Southern Opet; the sea is the Great Green; and the fields of Ialu were the Egyptian version of our Paradise.

Since Egyptian names can be confusing, a list of the principal characters and gods in the story can be found at the end of the book.

PART 1
PRINCESS

CHAPTER 1

*Year 9 of the Reign
of His Majesty Thutmose I*

How I detest this morning hour set aside for *readying our person.* It is not amusing to be readied.

Today is especially bad. Pekey, Mother's maid, who is supposed to be an artist with cosmetics, takes out all her enormous spite on me. Like a farmer with a sharp plow, she digs the comb into my scalp, raking up ridges of skin. With relish she concocts tangles which must be yanked out. Dabs kohl in my eyes. Scrubs a cleansing cream of chalk and oil into my cheeks till they sting like scorpion bites. And all the while she coos, "Ah, she is beautiful as the morning star! Such a complexion . . ." so that the serving women will believe she admires me.

Take care, Pekey. I will get even for every dig, yank, and sting, be assured. Ow! You will regret *that* tangle, pig.

My nurse, Henut, enters the scene, calm, unctuous. She surveys Pekey's smug face, my sulky one. Have I offered my morning's thanks to Amon-Re, she wishes to know. Gratitude unending is due from me and my brothers, the most fortunate beings in the world.

I stare at her, unblinking as a cobra. "Fortunate? Why?"

Henut swells like a pigeon, happy at the opportunity to preach. "Ah! You ask? To be born Egyptian is immense fortune. No one will argue it."

Well, of course not, everyone has that much sense.

She rattles on. "To be a member of the most powerful, beautiful, healthy country on earth. To be royalty. To belong to a great dynasty, with a father who is God-King, a mother who is Great Queen, two princes for brothers, and you yourself a princess." She stops for breath.

No more—I know the rest by heart. I live in the finest dwelling in Egypt, the Great House; I eat delicate food, dress in elegant clothing, wear spectacular jewelry. At thirteen years of age I can do—almost—anything in the world I wish to do.

I consider. Possibly Henut is right. What more could I want?

Oh, I decide, a good deal more. I am not *completely* fortunate. After all, I am a girl.

"Not true," Henut would retort. "In Egypt the line of succession passes through women, not men."

"The line of succession is boring."

"You are easily bored," Henut says with a sigh. "And restless. Ay, you are restless."

And why not? If I were a boy I could shoot arrows and row a boat and drive a chariot and swim. One day I could be a soldier and lead men in expeditions against the vile foreigners, as my father does.

"Ow!" Pekey has wielded the pumice stone with such vigor that she draws blood. I return to the present, suck my finger, and glare. She simpers.

What do I expect? She is a slave, a Nubian princess captured in battle. From royalty to servant is a far fall, and she resents it. Nevertheless, that is not my fault. My scratched finger I add to the score I will repay. I brood. And suddenly I conceive my revenge.

Waiting until Henut has left the room, I ask in a low, confidential voice, "Why is it, Pekey, you are always sent to help with my makeup? Henut says you apply kohl much too lavishly, so that one is left looking like a dancing girl."

Pekey's face lengthens at the affront. "Now, Your Highness, I make up your own mother the Great Queen's face. . . ."

"Using so much color on the cheeks that she appears to have a fever."

There is silence while Pekey putters with my equipment, the bronze mirror with the ivory handle, palettes of ground malachite for the eyes, ocher for the lips and cheeks, and an enormous assortment of small jars and unguent spoons. There is even a pair of boxwood containers in the form of two Asiatic maids carrying jars. They belong to Mother and hold perfumed oils. I drum my heel on the floor. "Well, let us continue, Pekey. As is said everywhere, you work slowly. We must waste no more time."

The lesser maids are holding their breath. They look scandalized. At me or at Pekey?

"I have never heard I am slow . . . Highness." Pekey is recovering.

My voice is firm and cool. "I have heard so. From superior sources." (A lie; Mother praises Pekey's technique to the skies.) "It is not a grave fault. Merely an annoying one."

Pekey does not answer. As she mixes ocher to rouge my lips, I see her fingers tremble. Ah, she begins to believe me! Now, wretch, you will suffer, you will for once doubt your skill, you will not be so sure your mistress trusts you. Indeed, I will get even for your petty persecutions.

And then . . . I feel a painful, terrible remorse for hurting someone. It is always the same. I can be rude and ruthless and cruel to a person I dislike, but if he betrays his wounds, my heart shivers as though stroked by a cold knife and I despise myself.

I sigh. "It is all a joke, Pekey."

"Joke, Princess?" She massages the color into my face and neck, and her eyes will not meet mine.

"Yes, yes, it is all untrue what I said. I did it to tease you. Henut and everyone say only good things about your makeup."

7

Still rubbing in the grease, Pekey asks softly, "You do not like me, young mistress?"

Oh, how tiresome! Why do I ever start such silly tricks when they end so lamentably?

"Yes, I *do* like you, Pekey." Actually I hate her, but now I am caught like a heron in a snare. I must lie to give her comfort and to ease my guilt.

Luckily Henut comes in to fit on my wig. This is a complicated affair of thin snaky black plaits interspersed with strings of gold beads. It is supposed to be a protection for my head, neck, and shoulders against the warmth of an already scorching day.

Pekey finishes brushing paint on my face and now rubs henna on my palms and the soles of my feet. She works briskly, and I hope she has forgiven me.

"There, Henut, does she look like a dancing girl?" Pekey's voice is innocent, but Henut's eyes are shocked.

"Dancing girl? Dancing girl! Her Majesty . . ."

Pekey gathers up the boxwood cosmetic figures and glides from the room—the victor.

Henut's face is stricken. "She meant no harm, Highness, but I shall report . . ."

"No, Henut. It was all . . . sort of a joke. We had been talking of dancing girls."

Yes, I am a princess, I reflect, one of the most powerful personages in the Two Lands. And what good is my power against a poor slave? I could order her whipped or her hands cut off (if Mother would agree)—and my regret would strangle my heart. What ails me? I am daughter and granddaughter of pharaohs; stern, just, resolute, courageous men who would brook no hint of insult or impertinence. Well. I must develop resolution. I must develop resolution. I must devel—

"Well?" Henut speaks impatiently. Really, she shows insufficient respect for a royal princess. It appears I am finally readied.

Attired in my white linen robe and soft sandals, with little jewelry because of the heat, I escape the room. Gorgeously painted and brushed and plucked, I am ready to . . . attend my lessons.

"Fortunate, fortunate me," I murmur. Lessons!

Father's own scribe, Tutami, teaches my brothers Wadjmose and Amenmose and me to read and write, not just the old formal style, but the new as well. They are both as boring as the line of succession, and I complain to my mother, who knows neither reading nor writing.

"Thy father insists upon it. It is part of being a princess," she says mildly.

"But why? Thou didst not learn them. Besides, scribes do the writing for us."

"I have on occasion wished for the skill. One day thou mayst wish to communicate with someone who is not close by. And thou mayst not wish thy thoughts to be known to others."

It seems a farfetched reason. But if Father desires it, that is cause enough. Father is the greatest God-King who has ever lived. And he is wise.

So I reconcile myself to lessons. Writing demands the most effort. For forming the glyphs—harder and more time-consuming than the practical hieratic writing, but they are decorative—we use boards covered with gesso. This is because Tutami prides himself on being economical. He tells us rambling stories of his boyhood and how he had only broken bits of pottery to write on, and are we not fortunate to have smooth boards for practice? *Fortunate* again. I am sick of the word.

For special exercises we are alloted a sheet of papyrus each. However, our too-conscientious teacher decides we must first learn how paper is made. We groan inwardly, but the process unexpectedly turns out to be interesting.

Papyrus plants, growing in the marshes, are selected carefully, not too old and stiff, not too young and green. The stalks are peeled and the pith cut into thin strips. The strips are laid lengthwise on a long stone table, then more strips are laid crosswise over the first layer. Next, with a wooden mallet the strips are pounded until the material is flattened into a sheet. This is then burnished with a stone tool to a shiny smoothness. For long documents sheets are fastened end to end and then rolled.

"I myself worked for a time in a papermaker's shop," Tutami informs us. "My hands were always grazed and cut from the pith, my arms ached from hammering, my back from burnishing. Indeed, young princes and princess, paper should never be wasted on mere ordinary practice."

During Tutami's lecture, Wadjmose has sketched a

very ugly portrait of our teacher. Unfortunately, instead of chalk he has used a black stone whose mark cannot be wiped off. Tutami, with his keen eyes (four all together, two in the back of his head), spies the picture and snatches the board.

"Aha!" he exclaims, gazing at it. "A self-portrait, Wadjmose?" He gazes from my brother to board and back. "Not bad, not bad, you have caught the essence of yourself."

Wadjmose blushes and Amenmose snickers. One seldom gets the better of Tutami.

Along with reading and writing, we study literature and history and some mathematics. The latter is a subject we three are stupid at.

When we grumble, Tutami speaks severely. "Without mathematics how could the great pyramids or the innumerable temples of the Two Lands have been constructed? Or the marvelous labyrinthine temple of King Ammenemes III?"

"But *we* as kings will not build pyramids or temples," Amenmose protests in his priggish manner. "We will command others to build them."

"Ah, will you know *how* to command, *what* to command, *whom* to command? Mathematics teaches one precision, reason, logic. It is a civilized science." Under Tutami's cold glance Amenmose subsides.

Soon after, we begin our history lesson. I dearly love history, studying our long line of kings, at the beginning of which was King Narmer, who, some sixteen hundred years ago, unified Upper and Lower

Egypt. The core of the Two Lands is the Nile; a map shows it like a lotus, the stalk extending up through the desert to the Great Green, where the branches form the blossom. For centuries we have been the greatest country of the world, and never so great as now.

My father, Thutmose I, a mighty warrior, has extended the boundaries of Egypt from the Horns of the Earth to the Marshes of Asia.

My great-grandfather was Ahmose, who began our dynasty. It was he with his brother, Kamose, who drove the vagabond Hyksos out of the country and again united Upper and Lower Egypt after two hundred years of chaos. Ahmose was a pharaoh to admire, respect, and revere, says my father. Naturally, for without him Father would not exist, nor would I.

But I am not grateful for mere existence. A dog exists. And a snake. I am going to do more than exist; I will make an art of existing, as Pekey makes an art with her cosmetics. Only I shall be a true artist.

As a soldier Father was an artist. I learned more about him last night at a banquet here at the palace. Since I was there without permission, I folded myself like a fan on a small corner of couch behind a bulky cushion to watch and listen. The Vizier was there, a dry little man with a twitch in one eyelid, and Captain Panakht, along with other military and government officials.

The Captain is my favorite tale-teller, although not the best. I mean by that that he sees himself back in the action of war and speaks feelingly of exciting exploits. However, he being a hearty but shy man and not easy with words, his descriptions come out in puffs and explosions. Last night he described a battle against the Nubians, when he had accompanied Father on a warship up the Nile.

"The water . . . the water there above the third cataract . . . was rough . . . rough like those wretched barbarians we came to fight. . . ." He shakes his head.

"Not civilized . . . I mean the people . . . the river, too. . . . It acquires civilization as it moves north. . . . But that day our fleet . . . with the sails bulging . . . and the planks creaking . . . the oars moving to the notes of the flutes . . . like singers to a leader . . . and soldiers balanced on the decks . . . with their huge bows ready . . ." Here he stops, out of breath, and gives a wild cough and draws his sleeve across his perspiring face.

"And His Majesty himself, Amon protect him . . . striding up and down . . . his guard pushed back against the rope . . . to give him room. . . . Ah, His Majesty was angry . . . raging like a panther . . . impatient to fight . . . and then suddenly at sunrise . . . around an island . . . appear the ships . . . our Nubian enemies' ships. . . . And all the men call out, 'Ayyyyyy!' . . . but His Majesty says nothing . . . only leans over the ropes . . . looking and looking. . . .

"And he spies it! . . . Spies it before I . . . I who am—was—called Eye-of-the-Hawk . . . as you know. He sees the enemy's flagship . . . cries to me . . . 'Yonder!

Leftward, quickly!' and then . . . 'Clear the way, all!' . . . He pulls an arrow, fits it to his tall bow, draws, aims . . . and all the while the ship . . . strains and tugs like a nervous horse. . . ."

The Captain coughs again, stares about as though to wonder how he came to be in the banquet hall rather than on the ship. For a moment he is confused, forgets the story.

Someone prompts him. "The river is rough, but His Majesty aims and . . . ?"

"Aims . . . oh yes, aims . . . standing there at the bow . . . imperious and wonderful, like the figurehead of Amon's sun boat . . . ah, he is the pharaoh of all pharaohs . . . there was none, will be none . . . to equal him. . . ."

Everyone in the hall bows his head in agreement, but still all are impatient. The Captain, however, cannot be rushed. He coughs, somehow gets himself back in time and place, becomes again Commander of the Egyptian fleet.

"He releases the arrow . . . which flies straight as the rays of Amon . . . to the breast of the Nubian chieftain . . . killing him . . . and the battle is over. . . . All ships submit . . . the vile foreigners shrieking and wailing . . . as vile foreigners always do . . . and by Pharaoh's command . . . we fasten the chieftain head downward . . . to the prow of our ship . . . for the homeward journey. And so decorated . . . we sailed to No-Amon. . . . How the people cheered him!"

He sinks back against a cushion, more exhausted from storytelling than from commanding a battle. My brothers roll their eyes at each other. They consider the Captain outworn and dated, a fuddy-duddy.

I like his bluffness, his honesty, even his awkwardness of speech. Above all, I like him for his admiration of my father, for, as he said, Thutmose is pharaoh of pharaohs, with none ever to equal him. Were I a prince, I would choose the Captain to serve me, too.

The Vizier, not to be outdone, is preparing to speak. This he does by rising, expanding his chest, gazing intently at everybody around him, and raising his hand as signal of a momentous announcement. His eyelid is leaping like a cricket with excitement.

"May I remind you"—his deep voice comes as a surprise, the most impressive thing about him—"that illustrious Pharaoh"—here he bows to Father so that everyone else has to rise and bow as well—"not only conquered our traditional enemies the Nubians but even more valiantly led Egypt's armies all the way to the far Great River of Syria! Recall further: His lance was as accurate as his arrow. He defeated the wretched Asiatics and took many prisoners."

Again he gazes fiercely about him as if awaiting an objection. Really he is a comical man. Him I would *not* have as vizier if I were king.

If I were king . . . what an intriguing, wonderful, impossible dream. Oh well, resolution, Hatshepsut. Life is before thee. Reflect on the words of that ancient poem Tutami is forever quoting:

Put myrrh upon thy head,
And garments on thee of fine linen,
  . . .
Increase yet more thy delights,
And let not thy heart languish.
Follow thy desire and thy good,
Fashion thine affairs on earth
After the mandates of thine own heart.

The mandates of my own heart. What are they? Well . . . I will hope, hope, hope . . . and I will pray to Hathor and to great Amon-Re and I will give them offerings, and I will hope more—that someday I will have the opportunity to do something splendid, to serve my Egypt, to show the world that I am not only fortunate but also worthy. We will see.

Anyway, tomorrow begin our holidays for the New Year and the Festival of Amon-Re. No lessons for an entire month!

CHAPTER 2

Year 10 of the Reign
of His Majesty Thutmose I

Today is the Feast of Opet and the Festival of Amon-Re, god of No-Amon. The cult of Amon is the official state religion of our royal family. I think of Amon as a stern and majestic father, but for the small things I desire I pray to Hathor, goddess of love and beauty. Surely she is more tender and yielding than Amon-Re.

How I detest festivals. For someone so fortunate, I seem to detest any number of things.

Henut says I am peculiar, since everybody in Egypt except me adores festivals. The reason is that I cannot look at the celebration but, being part of it, must be looked *at*. Then of course I receive lectures from my mother and Henut about obliging the common people and being happy that they are happy, etc. Well, I will just sift as much happiness as I can for myself from the day.

The hour of being readied is more harrowing than usual because Pekey is silent and cool instead of gushy, but as malicious as ever in the matters of tugging, raking, scouring, and bruising. I say nothing. Already my resolution is expanding.

Henut shoves my arms into a new robe, white, bordered with a broad blue band, the pleats so full of starch I might as well wear a box. A maid switches it around me, pins it with a gold scarab dotted with garnets. My neck is sheathed in a wide collar of gold filigree set with turquoise, my arms with bracelets of gold and faience, and my ankles with colored beads shaped like flowers. I am a prisoner wearing jeweled fetters.

"I shall die of the heat," I mutter. "There is nothing cool about jewelry."

Henut puts into my hands a red leather case holding my feathered fan. "This will cool you," she says cheerfully. Her work done, she will watch the procession from the shade of a palace terrace. No wonder she is cheerful.

Pharaoh, my mother, my brothers, and I are escorted to the royal barge, seated in cushioned chairs on the deck. Two little Nubians are set to fan us with huge ostrich-feather fans while we await the sacred barge of Amon.

The Nubian boys are young—about eight, I imagine. They are so fearful of being caught gazing at Pharaoh that they keep their heads bowed tightly against their chests. Naturally, with their eyes closed or focused on their feet, they cannot see what they are doing. One fan scrapes my brother Amenmose. Angrily he shoves fan and child, and a guard hastily removes both. Well, Amenmose is simply being resolute. Take note, Hatshepsut.

Horns sound. Amon's barge approaches. The chattering people on the riverbanks hush and bow their heads. So do we. Amon is god of gods, and he travels today from Ipet-Isut to Southern Opet to spend a month with his wife and son. The floods are at their height, and since the farmers have nothing to do, they welcome a festival. Actually, they welcome one at any time.

Amon's divine barge is a floating temple decorated with gold, silver, and lapis lazuli, its high prow and stern carved in the form of rams' heads, the hull covered with bas-reliefs. Amidships, shaded by a canopy and flanked by miniature obelisks, stands the ebony shrine that houses the image of Amon.

Only the priests see the image, for it must be "less accessible than that which is in heaven, more secret than the affairs of the nether world, more hidden than the inhabitants of the primeval ocean." My brother Wadjmose says the image is of gold set with precious gems, but this is hearsay, as *he* has never seen it.

The god is accompanied by priests. I recognize the High Priest by the panther skin draped over his white tunic. They all chant solemn hymns to Amon while priestesses shake their sistrums.

"High Priest appears very serious for such a joyful occasion," I whisper to Wadjmose.

"It is a grave and momentous event," he whispers back. Wadjmose is pompous and has no sense of humor. Still, he is more likable than Amenmose, who has no humor but plenty of temper—which trait he shares with me. I wonder which of them my father will designate as his successor. I do not look forward to the rule of either. Wadjmose would be dull and Amenmose arrogant.

The royal barges follow those of Amon and are towed up the Nile by barges equipped with sails. Swarms of colorful little boats accompany them, weaving about one another to form a bright tapestry. The spectators lining the banks laugh and clap their hands rhythmically and wave banners, as excited by the entertainers as by the procession.

Among the crowd, dancing girls in transparent skirts clap and twirl and turn cartwheels. Men beat tambourines. I catch sight of soldiers blowing trumpets; they wear feathers in their hair like foreigners. Refreshment tents and booths are set up all along the banks, selling beer and pastries, watermelon and strips of roast oxen.

"I am hungry," I announce to the world at large.

Two servants explode to my side, loaded with trays of wine and dried figs and my favorite date cakes. Actually I am enjoying the festival far more than I thought I would. Amenmose blows a melon seed at Wadjmose. Mother frowns at such irreverence; Pharaoh does not see—or pretends not to. He is always indulgent with us.

The rest of the day should pass as pleasantly. Pharaoh and my mother will give a reception for the foreign diplomats this evening, but I am excused from that as well as from the banquet. So are my brothers. Mother makes the excuse that we would be too tired to attend; the real reason is that practically all the guests will get drunk. They will become silly, be sick over the floor, and have to be carried home. Father does not approve of this lack of decorum; he is fastidious about public behavior.

Ahead, the temples of Southern Opet glow with rich colors, their flagpoles bright with bunting. On reaching the dock, our royal family parades at a stately gait from the quay to the temple of Mut and Chons, Amon's wife and son. Amenmose and Wadjmose are as usual bent on impressing the crowd and join in the religious hymns with pretentious fervor. I mold a rapt expression on my face, but when my sandal catches on a stone, nearly tearing off my big toe, the rapture dissolves.

What would happen were Pharaoh to trip and break his sandal? Would the Royal Keeper of the Sandals be summoned to repair or replace them in front of the multitude? (The multitude is supposed to keep their eyes downcast before Pharaoh, but occasionally they peek—I have seen them.) But no, Amon would never permit such a mishap to occur.

Wearily we ascend the steps of the temple. It is the

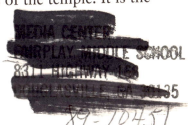

MEDIA CENTER
FAIRPLAY MIDDLE SCHOOL
8311 HIGHWAY 166
LOUISVILLE, PA 17135

89-10451

one ceremony of the year when the royal family, including Pharaoh, walks rather than having itself borne in litters. Thus we pay homage to Amon, Mut, and Chons. Being unused to walking, I have worn blisters on my feet—ow, how they sting—and I must still walk *back* to the barge.

We gather about the altar to witness the ritual of sacrifice to Amon. I close my eyes and wish I could close my ears as a huge ox is slaughtered before us. To take my mind off the act, I peer around me. In addition to the immediate family, Pharaoh's entire harem, with offspring, is present. Mother surely finds the sight offensive, although she gives no sign. In her place I would not put up with it: I would insist that the harem take a back position to the true family.

My heart gives a lurch. As Pharaoh, my father, observes the sacrifice, his hand is on the head of a boy—a puny, ugly boy—of roughly my age. Thutmose II! I feel faint and sick. Must he demonstrate his affection towards that one at such a time? God-King or not, he has no right. . . . No, no, I mean no irreverence, only . . . The boy is my half-brother, Pharaoh's son by a lesser queen, Mutnofre.

Mutnofre stands near me, her eyes on Pharaoh and the boy, a little smile on her face. For my mother's sake, for my own, I hate her; I should like to drop poison in her wine or push her into the river, into the jaws of a crocodile or . . . Control thy temper, Hatshepsut! As Mother admonishes us, a king and queen must be in perfect command of themselves always.

My eyes meet those of Amenmose and I see we share the same thought. He scowls at the sickly, pale Thutmose II. Pharaoh has the right to name his own successor, legitimacy or age having no bearing. What if he should designate Thutmose? He is partial to the boy—why, I do not understand, homely and weak and spiritless as he is.

An unendurable thought comes to me: Should he be named the next pharaoh, I would have to marry him. My divine and royal blood would make his position secure. No! I would refuse, I would drink nightshade. It cannot happen, I am imagining things. Pharaoh is merely showing pity for the boy, or the fondness one feels for a kitten. Hathor, dear goddess, let this be so!

At last the ritual comes to an end. "It was well done, was it not?" Wadjmose asks.

I shrug, having noticed little of it. "Yes, quite well."

Amenmose broods. "The ceremony is too crowded. Better to be limited to fewer priests and the true royal family."

"It is," remarks Wadjmose in surprise.

"The *immediate* family," says Amenmose impatiently. "Pharaoh; our mother, the Great Queen; and us three."

"Well, yes." Wadjmose is as usual agreeable. Too agreeable. Resolution would suit him better. Since of him, Amenmose, and Thutmose, he would be my choice to succeed to the throne—a sad choice in any case—I must work on his character.

23

"Concubines and lesser queens and princes should be excluded," I say firmly. "Surely thou canst see that, Wadjmose."

"Y-yes." He looks uneasy.

"*I* would abolish the harem," I go on. "It complicates matters."

"The harem is an established institution," Amenmose states coldly. I decide that I do not like him much better than Thutmose.

Now the priests are commencing a performance of Amon's struggles against some of the minor gods. It is acted with a good deal of energy by apprentice priests, accompanied by a chorus with voices like trumpets. My ears are weary from loud noises; my eyes rebel at so much restless movement and color; my nose is tired of breathing in dust and sweat and ammonia, terebinth and scorched cakes and cloying incense.

The ceremony is nearly over. Pharaoh strides from the gilded chair to kneel before the shrine of Amon to give thanks for a plentiful inundation this year. Reports have already arrived that the god of the Nile, Hapi, the bringer of food, rich in provisions, creator of all good, has granted us a better-than-average one, and the summer will be good.

Flood is my favorite season. We have picnics on our barge, with cold roast dove and hare and cucumber salad and cool wine. While we eat, wrestlers and clever jugglers and fine musicians entertain us. Last year there were two acrobats, young boys; one of them

24

could stand on his head and balance the other on his feet. Both could do handsprings without touching the ground. Later at home Wadjmose attempted to copy the act and landed square on his back.

Pharaoh rises from his knees. He and my mother are carried back to the barge, but the rest of us walk. I turn my head and find myself eye to eye with Mutnofre. She smiles, and I ignore her. This time there will be no remorse; I can become very resolute when I think of possible marriage with Mutnofre's son, that wan weakling. I must do all possible to promote Wadjmose with Father. This will not be difficult. He favors me, I believe, even above Thutmose II.

Resolution was not enough. During the season of sowing, Wadjmose was swimming in the river with Amenmose and two lesser princes, when he became entangled in weeds without anyone seeing, and drowned. Two months later Amenmose suddenly fell ill with lung fever; in only three days he was dead. My mother was beside herself, and Pharaoh was grim and silent; he spent much time in his private sanctuary, praying to Amon.

Perhaps he felt the death of his sons was a warning to him. He quickly named Thutmose II as his successor and made arrangements for our marriage. I was too numb to argue. But time after time there comes to mind Henut's remark that Amenmose, Wadjmose, and I are the most fortunate beings in the Two Lands. Wrong, wrong, wrong, Henut! My brothers are no more, and I am to marry that flabby creature.

But *I* am not flabby—I am as healthy as he is sickly, and he will not find me easy to bend or break. Only now my temper sickens and flares, so that I strike—at officials, at servants, at any member of the harem. Mutnofre I do not allow near me, nor will I ever, even after I am married to her son.

I have become, once and for all, resolute. No longer will events or people control me as heretofore. From now on I will control *them*. Marry Thutmose I must, but that is the last time I will do anything unless *I, Hatshepsut, wish to do it.*

Two days after the marriage I change from Princess to Great Queen, and my husband to Great God Pharaoh Thutmose II, King of Upper and Lower Egypt. My father, on his return home from an inspection of his tomb—the first to be tunneled in a remote valley, so the trip was long and tiring—stepped from his barge onto the palace quay, gave a terrible grimace, and fell to the ground. As no one touches Pharaoh without permission except the Steward of the Dress, this one had to be sent for, along with the doctor. They pronounced my father dead.

There was no sign of poison, nothing abnormal, the doctors assured me. Thutmose II appeared ready to collapse with grief but managed, to my surprise, to remember the duties of a God-King. Perhaps he remembered that by performing the burial rites of his father, he confirmed his right to the throne. At any rate, he ordered a funeral worthy of a pharaoh. Of a warrior-pharaoh.

Father's old friend Lord Ineni, Chief Architect of the King, had been in charge of quarrying the tomb. As tombs go, it is smallish, consisting of an antechamber at the foot of steep stairs, the sepulchral hall, and a storeroom, all hewn out of rock.

Ineni wrote: "I saw to the digging of the hill-sepulcher of His Majesty privily, none seeing and hearing." I hope that is true, so that his *ka*, or soul, with the help of paintings, *shabtis,* and equipment, and daily food offerings, may continue its existence in peace and happiness, safe from the accursed tomb robbers.

Today, after praying in Amon's chief temple for Father's successful meeting with Osiris in the Underworld, I visit our old nursery. Henut, who has risen from nurse to my chief maid, is packing toys into chests. There is my beautiful doll Kawit, with her long beaded hair and her little gold cup, and the red leather ball, and the two ivory dwarfs that dance on a baseboard when you work their strings. And there is Wadjmose's wooden top and his set of soldiers with their movable heads.

Henut asks, "Do you wish them left out, Majesty? Your doll Kawit—will you take her with you?"

I shake my head. My childhood is over, and I put it behind me. One of the most fortunate beings in the world I may be. If so, I shudder at the lot of unfortunates.

27

PART 2
QUEEN

CHAPTER 3

Year 13 of the Reign
of His Majesty Thutmose II

For thirteen years I have been "Daughter of the King, Sister of the King, Wife of the God, and Great Royal Wife Hatshepsut."

The most startling aspect of our marriage is my recent realization that my God-King husband dislikes me almost as much as I dislike him. Startling to me, I mean, and disconcerting as well. For what has he to complain of? Of all the blood in Egypt, mine is the most royal, the most divine; in marrying me he ensured himself the pharaohship. What more could he ask?

I bore him two daughters, Ahotep and Nefrure, the first dying at two years, the other bright and beautiful. When Thutmose is sickly—which is often—I take over a few of the regal duties, thus provoking the Vizier, that snotty little man with the twitch, who tries to disguise a pained expression whenever I address him. (My husband considers him indispensable—a ridiculous idea, since no one is indispensable.) I have seen to the repair and refurbishing of the Great House, surely a woman's prerogative, although my husband was annoyed that I did not consult him on a few minor changes.

Oh yes, and most importantly, I have closely supervised the mortuary rites for our father. It is not that my husband is exactly remiss in this, but being unhealthy, he spares himself.

"I am aware of my father's needs in the Eternal," he states pompously. "I have paid good gold to the temple of Amon to provide fresh food for his *ka* each day. Why must thou interfere?"

"Because thou dost not check the High Priest's assurance that the food has indeed been offered. I am not so trustful of promises as thou."

"Thou trustest none of my officials. Moreover, thy distrust is evident." He coughs wearily and glares at me, resentful of my health and vitality.

Why then does he not forbid my interference? My father, with one imperious gesture, would have done so. Pharaoh is all-powerful. None may dispute him. But I dispute Thutmose II constantly, even occasionally with malice, and for this I feel no remorse at all. I, Hatshepsut, have truly become resolute.

In the first years of our marriage Thutmose behaved, surprisingly, as a king should behave. There arrived news of an insurrection in Nubia:

"One hastened to deliver to His Majesty the news that vile Cush had revolted, that certain of those subjects of the Lord of the Two Lands had plotted to plunder the people of Egypt and to steal cattle. Already a chieftain of that vile Cush along with his two sons were in a state of rebellion."

Thutmose became red as a radish, raged up and down the room, and threatened to kill every Nubian in Cush. He was so royally wrathful that for the first time I liked him, even admired him.

He marched off at the head of his army, whipped Nubia soundly, and lopped off the heads of the rebelling chieftain and his children, all but one. That one he brought back to No-Amon to clean the latrines and floors of the palace. And he left on the road between Aswan and Philae a triumphal monument of his victory.

In Palestine he did the same thing, taking many prisoners while crushing a revolt. The prisoners are useful, he maintains, either as household servants or as hewers of rock tombs or even as soldiers. *But*, I argue, all possess mouths which must be filled twice a day from Egypt's granaries. More profitable it might have been to leave their bodies in Palestine.

Since those expeditions, however, my husband has forsaken military life for the sick bed, with some riotous living thrown in. Luckily for Egypt, this has been a time of peace and the willing payment of tribute. Otherwise, news of an ailing king might tempt the wretched foreigners to another of their uprisings.

33

I sometimes speak of my father to Henut, who always fervently admired him.

"Oh, Majesty, he was truly a warrior-pharaoh," she remarks, hands on hips, during a pause from fussing among the inlaid boxes and cosmetic jars on my table. Henut can never stand or sit still for more than a moment. She must constantly be in motion.

"The greatest of warrior-pharaohs," I add. "There lack sufficient monuments to his greatness, Henut. Were I Pharaoh I should have many more constructed up and down the Nile."

Henut frowns slightly. She holds her tongue, but I can guess what she is thinking: This Great Queen Hatshepsut has changed not a jot from that restless, discontented, critical little Princess Hatshepsut. Well, why should I? Nothing else has changed.

"The present Pharaoh, our Great God, is unwell." Muttering the excuse, Henut flaps her hands until she resembles a frightened duck. She dreads the candid remarks I make about my husband, expecting a guard suddenly to rise from the floor, take my arm, and lead me away to execution. He would have a hard time of it! Besides, Thutmose accepts my bluntness as few rulers would do.

"Who can doubt your father is well cared for in the Afterlife, Majesty?" Henut tries to soften my grumblings. "Pharaoh is pious and reveres his ancestors as much as you."

I shrug. "The High Priest of Amon is endowed for his lifetime, and his successor for *his* lifetime, to conduct services for my father, to place at his tomb fresh food daily. I shall see that they do so. But the following High Priest, having no memory of my father's greatness, may appropriate the money for himself. There is corruption everywhere, even in the priesthood."

"No, no, Majesty, never!" Henut cries, shocked. She clings to her dreams, convinced that only the poor are dishonest.

However, I myself have viewed abandoned tombs, looted tombs of remote pharaohs. Father was of the opinion such tombs could have been ferreted out and entered only with the connivance of the priesthood or high government officials, eager to fatten their grain bags or augment their herds of cattle. How else could the intruders avoid the false shafts, the doors set to drop and crush such criminals? How else could they tunnel through mountains of rock to arrive precisely at the burial chamber?

Some thieves have been caught and dealt with. They are not to be envied. But like ants, more appear to dare the wrath of Osiris for the sake of gold and treasure. Yet these are still fearful of the revenge of Pharaoh's *ka* and stop to gouge out the eyes of statues and reliefs so that the spirits may not spy them at their filthy work. With his image so maimed, Pharaoh's soul may languish and die the second and final death.

Resolution flows through me and I set my jaw. "Be assured, Henut, that at least for my lifetime Father's tomb will be safe."

My lifetime. How long will that be? More important than quantity of years is their quality, and so far, for me that is not high. I, who had intended to mold myself into beauty and strength as Khnum, god of creation, molds persons and souls on his potter's wheel. I, who have always felt that my life was reserved for something splendid, something important for the Two Lands. What illusion.

CHAPTER 4

My days pass like beads on a necklet, all uniform, each one the same shiny blue, slipping round and round in a dull circle. I prod my husband to build for Egypt, fight for Egypt, form laws, change laws, seek out injustice and punish it. On his better days he pats my arm and smiles slightly; on his worse ones he glares like a panther and growls like one, and I thank Hathor that Egypt is too civilized to permit the murder of wives.

I possess no more power than a pet monkey or a slave girl, not so much if she is pretty. My husband has a weakness for soft, fluffy girls. What was that Henut said years ago? I am the most fortunate of beings, being born a princess. Ha! A princess may feel as helpless as a peasant. So may a queen.

But I forget how quickly life can change.

Yesterday evening, the omens being favorable, my husband hosted a banquet. I repeat, the omens were favorable, the calendar day auspicious, the stars portended good luck; the soothsayers assured him of this. Only my own personal seer, old Bat, was cautious. After reading Thutmose's dream of a reptile emerging from water, he prophesied, "The day begins better than it ends." I paid little heed. Bat is always cryptic, always dreary, afraid on a clear day to predict the sun will shine.

Still, I tried to dissuade my husband. His favorite cat had scratched his upper arm and the wound had festered. How grave it had become I could not tell, for his Majesty treated it as nothing. Although the arm was bandaged, his sleeve hid the dressing. But his eyes glittered and his cheeks were flushed.

And so Pharaoh gave the banquet, inviting the usual officials, the usual foreign envoys, in particular the Syrian. To avoid arching the bow, Thutmose hosts a series of dull parties with the view of lulling the ambassadors into moderate friendliness and respect.

The Syrian envoy is as always obnoxious. With his greasy face and dirty beard and little piggy snout, he stares at each gold dish as he gulps its contents, openly longing to secrete it in his sash. What a one he is for gold, and all his people like him.

"Your Majesty"—he bows, those melon seeds he uses for eyes shrewd and appraising—"you do not accompany the Great God Pharaoh this year to inspect the boundaries?" Of course, he wishes to trick me into saying whether or not Pharaoh is well enough to attempt the journey.

I murmur a few words under my breath on purpose so he cannot understand me. From a passing servant I take a dish of pomegranates and offer him one. I hope it will be juicy enough to gush over his gaudy tunic.

The Vizier rescues me, taking the Syrian by the arm and leading him off as one would a cow. This is an innovation of my husband's, in which we leave our chairs for a time and mingle with the guests. It has its dangers, and one has just planted herself before me: the new wife of the Royal Treasurer, a young girl with bold eyes, now modestly downcast, and a pampered mouth. Her husband has urged her to gain my liking.

"Her Highness is magnificent tonight." She speaks in a breathy, affected voice. Her dress is as perfectly pleated as mine, her wig is of the latest fashion (not as high as mine, of course), her jewelry is eye-catching. But the wax cone of perfume on her head is soured, and gives off a sickly, rotted smell.

I nod graciously, holding my breath. "Watch these girls, they are quite good."

They are the best in Egypt, being Pharaoh's own dancing girls. There are ten of them, and in time to the clapping of musicians they kick high into the air, their anklets clacking, the heavy discs attached to their braids swinging wildly. Still in unison they slide into splits, then leap up and coil themselves into somersaults and backbends. An exotically tattooed girl jumps in and out of a hoop around which a number of daggers are fixed. Everyone gasps, expecting to see her slashed and bloody, but she is skillful and receives no injury.

"Indeed they are good! They are magnificent!" breathes the Treasurer's wife. Treasurer should work on her conversation—and her perfume.

"Such delicious food, the spiced pigeon, the honey cakes," she rattles on. "Truly Her Majesty's parties are magnificent!"

I am spared more. Thutmose's Steward of the Household, the one clever and amusing official in the palace, gently pushes the girl toward a group of women and guides me to an unoccupied corner.

"His Majesty's pet monkey has just made himself another enemy," he remarks lightly. "Ini reached down from the archway, yanked the wig off the Vizier's wife—revealing, by the way, a hideous growth on her scalp—swung back and forth a moment, waving the wig aloft for all to see, then dropped it neatly on the Libyan ambassador's head. The very ambassador who is so vain of his thatch of crinkly hair. Everybody clapped for joy."

I smile and think, Not everybody, not the lord my husband. He takes pains to keep his diplomatic family sweetly content, even the solemn Libyan and the greedy Syrian.

The Steward chatters on. "I begin to respect that Syrian. He has consumed some dozen cups of wine as thirstily as a laborer gulps water on a sweltering day, and still he stays sober as a judge."

"Which not everyone does." I wave toward a man, some minor state official from upriver, so tipsy the servants are escorting him outside. Once, only once, I saw my husband in that condition, after a small private dinner party. He was so ill the following day that he has never afterward drunk more than two cups of wine in an evening.

Now I glance about the room at the guests, at To the dwarf, who can turn somersaults and caper like a clown and at the same time sing like a bird, at the servants offering more sweet wine and almond cakes, at the golden thrones at one end of the room. There is no sign of Pharaoh.

"Have you seen His Majesty?" I ask.

The Steward sends me a stricken look. "I believe, Majesty, he felt weary enough to retire."

"Without sending word to me! That is uncommon."

"Suddenly unwell, Your Majesty. I expect he felt suddenly unwell." Steward appears uncomfortable, even hunted.

A suspicion shakes me. "Was anyone with him when he left?"

Perspiration drips down the Steward's face, and he blinks and squints like a toad. Oh, surely my suspicion is correct.

"One of the minor queens accompanied him, Majesty."

"Which concubine, Steward?" My tone is light, my face is calm, my breath slow, and inside, my heart rages like a lioness.

"Isis, Your Majesty." He is trying to match my mood—my exterior mood. But his mouth quivers, his eyes hold the panicked air of a deer about to flee for its life.

Isis! The entire court is aware of my loathing for her. I have never uttered a word against her—no one is more closemouthed than I—but my hatred I cannot disguise. She misses no opportunity to brag of her son as Thutmose's favorite. She even had the impudence to name him after my husband and after my father—Thutmose III.

What does my husband see in her? She has no intelligence, no culture or breeding, no beauty. Ah, she may be pretty in a common sort of way, but her features, the wide-set eyes, the thick brows, the soft, weak little mouth—she is a girl to suit an artisan, not a king! Thutmose demeans himself. He shows his own low breeding. He is a fool.

No, no, Hatshepsut, thou goest too far. Such thoughts are imprudent, even from thee. Besides, why should I care about a brazen concubine and a man whom I do not love?

"So then," I remark at length, keeping my voice casual. "Surely I will be informed if His Majesty is not well. Ah, here is Vizier. How went the hunting trip yesterday?"

The Vizier comes into quick bloom. "Well but well, Your Majesty! Three gazelles, fifty hares, quail without number . . ." He boasts as though he were the only hunter in Egypt, his silly eyelid fluttering like a moth.

I see to it that neither he nor anyone else thinks me anything but indifferent to Isis—except the Steward, who is more perceptive than most. And what he senses he will keep to himself. What a stupid institution, the harem! Of some use politically, but a bed of gossip and intrigue, every concubine maneuvering her children to Pharaoh's attention.

I blink. Vizier stares at me, a silly smile on his face.

"You say, Vizier?"

"I do not see His Majesty. I trust he is not ill?"

"As you know, His Majesty soon tires of social occasions. . . . Your family is well, the children in the country?"

The Vizier blathers on. My mother hated the harem of Thutmose I, despised the little harem boy who is now my husband. I despise the son of Isis, that little prig with his watchful eyes. Hatshepsut! Calm thyself. He is . . . what? Eight or nine years old? At any rate, no threat to thee. Children constantly contract diseases, have accidents . . .

Titters, smiles. Vizier has just made an entertaining remark (for him) and is beaming at me. I manage to look amused.

All at once I am weary enough to weep . . . to

faint . . . to die. More and more Henut's words ring through my head: You are the most fortunate being in the world. Oh, would that I possessed power and could leave the fortunate to someone else. I am the most sensible person at court, I know what should be done—and I have no more influence than a puppy to do it.

The acrobats file into the center of the ring. They are quite skilled, holding one another on their shoulders, doing two or three flips in the air. One can balance himself upside down on a man's head, using one hand.

This is my opportunity to retire, even if the guests believe me sulky because of Isis. I can bear no more of this foolish gaiety, these unremarkable people.

"Will you escort me to my chamber?" I ask the Steward. "My head begins to ache . . . from the noise and wine."

He throws up his arm as if I were a fat, dowdy old dowager queen. I lean on it as if in truth I were.

Now to find Pharaoh and inform him of alarmed questions from the guests on his condition. But just outside the great hall two guards rush up to me, kneel, and with agitation blurt out a few words.

"What is it?" I demand. "My daughter?"

"The Great God Pharaoh, Majesty. He is ill. The lady Isis summons you, the doctor is on his way, the High Priest is with him. We are to call the Vizier as well."

The Steward hurries to advise the Vizier. I walk quickly (but always with decorum) to my husband's apartment. He is stretched on his bed, eyes closed, his face pale and suffering, the sore arm exposed. Oh, that arm! It is swollen to a streaked gray and yellow, like the trunk of a tree. The High Priest bends over him, Isis crouches beside him, servants hover in corners, their faces like masks in the lamplight.

"Pharaoh needs air. Wait outside the door." I shoo the servants out. "You may go," I order Isis with hauteur. Slowly she rises, and hobbles out as though her legs are asleep.

The Vizier breaks through the linen door curtain. "His Majesty! His Majesty is not . . ."

Pharaoh's eyes open. I stoop so that our eyes are level.

"Does something pain thee? What dost thou need?"

He opens his mouth as though to grasp a breath that is not there. "My heart," he mumbles. "It is tired of . . . supporting this old shell . . ."

"The physicians come with medicines."

But Thutmose motions the Vizier to approach, pushes himself up on one elbow. His eyes moving from the High Priest to the Vizier, he states in a clear voice, "I name my successor as ruler of the Two Lands to be Thutmose III."

Isis's son. So he is, after all, a threat.

"And thou, Great Queen, wilt be his regent, wilt rule with him till he is old enough to do so alone."

He smiles faintly. "Thou art fully capable, Hatshepsut. Capable of guiding my son, of commanding the two kingdoms, until he is of age."

He falls back on the bed, his face tortured. The grotesque arm is extended as though he wishes to keep it as far away from himself as possible.

An hour later he is dead. After a period of uproar—the guests being ordered home, ambassadors milling in the courtyards, servants dashing aimlessly about like flocks of pigeons—the palace is quiet with shock.

Pharaoh is dead. Thanks be to Amon, he did not think to command the marriage of the Prince to our daughter, Nefrure. That will now never occur, I will see to that. The boy is not worthy, having only secondary royal blood in his body. In time he will be God-King of the Northern and Southern Kingdoms, of all Egypt, but at present he is a mere prince. And I am Queen-Regent.

The High Priest announces the death: "Year thirteen, fourth month of Harvest, day two. The god, His Majesty, has ascended to the Horizon. The Lord of the Two Lands has winged his way aloft to join himself with the sun's disc. The heart of the god has merged with the creator. The Great House is silent; hearts are in mourning; the gates of the City are barred; the nobles crouch head on knees; the grieving family weeps."

He likewise proclaims the usual seventy days of mourning for my husband. The court, envoys from all over the world, call at the palace to offer their condolences.

Henut eyes me strangely. "Do not hide your grief, Majesty. Display it before the world." Her tone is ironic. She knows how little moved I am by my husband's death.

I regret my lack of feeling. Thutmose was not a bad man or king. But always I knew myself more able—more kingly—than he.

Lord Ineni, expressing his condolences to me, says poetically, "The King rests from life, going forth to heaven, having completed his years in gladness of heart." I could have done much to make his heart more glad.

The High Priest requests an interview. "Is Her Majesty aware that our beloved Pharaoh has done little or nothing to ornament his tomb? He has never even planned his funerary temple!" His astonishment is evident.

Since my husband was still a young man, I am not so amazed. "I suppose he put off such decisions due to his illness and lethargy."

"The tomb he ordered hewn is small." The High Priest hesitates. "If Her Majesty has ideas on the subject . . . Perhaps she will take charge of completing the decoration, the furnishing?"

"I will see to it."

I will also see to those monuments to our father which my husband neglected to order built. He neglected much, Thutmose II.

For seventy days his body, with the organs re-moved, will be immersed in salt baths, then wrapped in layers of linen that have been soaked in pitch. Thus inured to time, the mummy is placed in the tomb, and his *ka* will be restored to second life by magic and ritual.

Essential are the daily offerings of fresh food that the *ka* has only to look at in order to gain sustenance. For comfort and entertainment Pharaoh must have his chair and bed and games with him. On the walls are painted those scenes that he most enjoyed in his first life, that his spirit may relive them. Since Thutmose did not himself choose which episodes most pleased him, I must do so. Hunting and boating scenes, campaign scenes, playing with his monkey Ini, scenes of dancing girls and musicians, will break the tedium of his House of Eternity. Of his family, only I and his daughters will be pictured. And there must be dozens of *shabtis*, those clay figures who will minister to Pharaoh in the Afterlife. The supervision of this will help occupy me during the dull time of mourning.

My daughter, Nefrure, comes to me, asking about her father. She is too young to understand death, but she has heard vaguely of Osiris and Judgment Day.

"What does it mean?" she asks.

"Thou knowest that Osiris is god of the dead. So when someone dies and enters the Underworld, Osiris must decide if he is good or bad."

"How can he decide?"

"Anubis, the jackal god who helps Osiris, weighs

the man's heart on one side of the scale, with the feather of truth on the other. If the scale balances true, the dead will be admitted to Eternity. Then it can dwell in the lovely fields of Ialu or it can flutter as a bird between the tomb and our own world."

"But if the person is bad?"

"He is devoured by a horrible monster with a crocodile head."

"And he cannot go to the Underworld?"

"That is right. Still, pharaohs, being godly, never fail the test."

Actually I do not feel certain of this. Does Osiris pardon ambition, greed, ruthlessness, self-indulgence? We will each find out in our own time.

The day of the funeral arrives. Thutmose's body, dressed in fine linen under the bandages and wearing a gold mask, is placed in an elaborately painted coffin, which is loaded onto a sledge drawn by members of his court. Following it is a line of servants who haul the carts of tomb furnishings. Among these is a dismantled chariot, the one my husband used in his Palestine campaign. Free of his ills, he may battle to his heart's content against the ghastly spirits of the Underworld.

The professional mourners outdo themselves in hysterical wailing. I cannot join their frenzy, even if I disappoint and shock the populace. Nefrure, holding my hand, is likewise solemn and untearful. Isis is doing her part, weeping gently—or timidly, as she does everything. Her son, marching beside me, keeps a stony face; he was, I am told, attached to his father. He is in no way attached to me. I mark his expressionless glances.

In a procession of boats we cross the river to the west bank, then regain our formation about Pharaoh's catafalque to the tomb. Here we must pause in the courtyard while the furniture and bric-a-brac are placed in the vault. Isis has worked herself into such a crying fit that she is disgracing herself. Eye makeup pours down her cheeks in streaks till she resembles a zebra.

Now the coffin vanishes down the dark steps, followed by only the priests, the Prince, and me. It is placed upright as the High Priest in his robe of leopard skin touches the sacred chisel to the lips of the face painted on the coffin; thus he "Opens the Mouth" and revives Pharaoh's senses. An assistant priest wears the jackal mask of Anubis; for a dizzy moment I feel that we have all entered the Underworld. With a quiver of apprehension I wonder if my husband can observe me now . . . can look into my heart and discover my indifference.

Finally the coffin is deposited in the red granite sarcophagus. As it is closed, the Prince tosses onto it a wreath of fresh flowers. The seals of the necropolis are set in the walls, and we escape up the steps. While the entrance is walled up by masons, we withdraw to the funeral feast.

Thanks be to Amon, this day is over. I confess I am untouched by deep grief, and yet I feel dreary and depressed. How else, after a visit to the tomb, after the finality of farewell to Thutmose? Whether I liked and loved him or not, we were man and wife for thirteen years. To my intense surprise, I find I miss him.

Enough of remorse, Hatshepsut! This is the time, if ever, for resolution.

CHAPTER 5

Year 2 of the Joint Reign
of His Majesty Thutmose III
and Her Majesty Queen-Regent Hatshepsut

The title "Joint Reign" is a foolishment and empha-
sizes what I have always contended: that men are more
fortunate than women.

Joint reign! It is *I* who inspects, examines, weighs,
and wrings her brain to a rag making decisions. The
Prince signs his name, is present at a few ceremonies
(where he yawns and writhes, driving everyone to
distraction), and spends the rest of his time swimming,
racing, wrestling, even whining to handle horse and
chariot. And still—on all documents, all letters, all
monuments, must be written "Joint Reign," his name
looming large as mine. A child of ten years. It is ridiculous.

All changes that I wish made must be introduced
with the utmost circumspection. Conservatism is the
byword of Egypt's history. To overturn any custom

is like opening a heavy door: A great deal of pulling and tugging is necessary, and then only the barest crack results.

I propose to the Third Priest of Amon (hesitantly, I admit, which is a mistake) that we replace the official soothsayer Bekt with a woman, Mekten.

"She is exceedingly accurate in her predictions," I end.

Third Priest dons his air of restrained patience. "Does Her Majesty recall that Bekt was appointed by Great Pharaoh Thutmose II? That Great Pharaoh found Bekt to be diligent and conscientious in his duties?"

"*I* find him fussing half the morning over his star charts, and then his predictions are mostly untrue."

The Third Priest is shocked and sees that he must take a firm stand. "Being female, this Mekten is incapable of such accuracy as Bekt." This is stated with cold conviction. As a sop to me, he adds, "To be Her Majesty's personal seer, Mekten would be most suitable."

For the moment I drop the matter. I am Queen-Regent, but any routine I wish to vary must be agreeable to my household steward *or* to the governing council *or* to the priesthood. Agreeable always to *men*.

However, I have accomplished some changes. The harem as such no longer exists. (Chief Steward admitted it was useless both to the Prince and to myself.) There, my husband—all thy simple, kittenish playfellows have been dispersed like weed fluff in the wind. Harem women are frivolous, uneconomical, and dangerous, with their dancing and chatter, their discordant music making and constant dressing of hair, their unending intrigues to further the interests of themselves and their children.

And so—daughters of minor foreign potentates have been returned to their lands; captive women have been freed or sold as slaves; relatives of nobles have been married off. Only those whose rejection would cause insult or embarrassment are allowed to remain in the palace—in apartments far removed from mine. The prime example is Isis, who as mother of the Prince is due a certain amount of respect, I suppose. At least for appearance's sake. Her rooms are located on the breezeless and sun-scorched side of the Great House.

I will say for her she does not complain. And if Thutmose II's *ka* visits the palace and notes the changes, it does not complain either. Surely his spirit is too occupied cavorting with other spirits to take notice of my alterations.

My daughter, who has moved from the nursery to my suite, grows more affectionate each day. Only with her can I relax—her and Henut. Nefrure is charming, already beautiful and graceful, with nice manners.

I relate to her bits of Egypt's history, myths and tales of the gods.

"Tell of Osiris," she begs.

I oblige. "Long ago lived Osiris, the earliest God-King of the Two Lands, who had taught his people agriculture and formed laws for their use. He had a wife, Isis, and a brother, Set. Set was very jealous of Osiris."

"Why? Why was he jealous?" Nefrure is puzzled by jealousy; she cannot yet understand the emotion.

"Because Set wished to be king in place of Osiris. So he tricked his brother into climbing into a chest. Then he clamped down the lid and threw the chest into the river. The good Osiris was drowned, but later Isis found the chest and body washed up on the shore of the Lebanon. Undergoing much hardship, she brought the body back to Egypt."

"Then Set came along," prompts Nefrure.

"Yes. Came along and stole the body and cut it up into pieces, which he scattered all over the Two Lands. Nevertheless, faithful Isis searched through the land until she had gathered together the fragments. These she fitted back together again and breathed life into the body. With the help of Thoth. Thoth is god of . . . ?"

"Scribes," Nefrure finishes promptly.

"*And* the moon. *And* wisdom. He is a mighty god, Thoth. Thutmose, the name of thy father and grandfather, means 'Child of Thoth.' "

Nefrure resents a story's turning into a lesson. "Go on, my mother. And Osiris?"

"Afterward Osiris and Isis had a son, Horus, who fought with Set and conquered him. Osiris became Lord of the Underworld, and Horus took his father's place as Pharaoh of Egypt. Ever since that time every King of the Two Lands is called 'the Horus.' "

shall prove worthy of your trust." He rises and backs from the room gracefully, unlike Dhose, who trips over his feet and leaves a trail of upset tables and stools and pedestals.

It is a small and unimportant event in a crowded day, but the episode buoys me up. Our court is made up of shrewd and efficient men: the Vizier and First Prophet of Amon, Hapusoneb (the old twitchy-eyed Vizier I retired after my husband's death); Chancellor Nuni; Chief Treasurer Kenut; and others. They are deliberate and as cautious as cats; there is nothing *bold* about any of them. Senmut, I suspect, possesses a daring streak—a refreshing quality in our conservative land. Moreover, if I reward his daring, *my* reward will be his loyalty . . . I hope.

Later in the day I find just reason to resent that caution of my good councillors, the Great Ones. At our daily meeting I first announce the appointment of Senmut as Overseer of Fields, an act that meets with fair approval. Dhose, when he hears of it, will be twice as ill as he is now and as furious as a bumblebee. Sad for him.

Next I broach the subject of Pharaoh's traditional tour of his lands. This circuit is supposed to be made once a year, as a sign to the entire world that Pharaoh is ever alert. Because of my husband's inertia, the expedition has not been made in more than five years. I intend to make it.

Council is upset, disgruntled, and horrified.

"Your Majesty . . . the tour is made only by a *king*."

"Such a trip is exhausting. Even for a youthful and healthy king."

"Foreign potentates do not expect a queen, or a regent, to follow tradition so closely. Trouble yourself not, Majesty—there will be no rude whispers among the diplomatic corps on *that* score."

Such nice dedicated gentlemen, all clucking indulgently at my feminine whims.

But what steels my determination is Treasurer's remark: "Oh, Your Majesty, in a year or so Prince Thutmose will be ready and eager for this duty."

Without thought my words explode sharp as the crack of a whip. "If a ten-year-old child is able to travel Egypt's boundaries, certainly a queen can do so. I find none of your objections valid."

There is much blinking and frowning and clearing of throats and shifting of eyes. They are clearly off-balance—the right moment to attack.

"Another matter. I wish to raise an obelisk in honor of my father, the Great God-King, in the temple of Amon."

With relief a chorus of assent pours over me; it is my consolation prize (they think). In the matter of monuments to our royal ancestors, agreement can be counted on. Tutami was right: Egypt likes nothing better than to build.

"I desire it accomplished with all speed. Vizier, can you begin the action at once?"

Again Treasurer's unctuous voice intervenes. "The order of work must be approved and signed by the approached my mother in the guise of Pharaoh, my father. Under the spell of the dream, I wax somewhat lyrical.

"He went to her, to the Great Queen Ahmose. He found her as she slept in the beauty of her palace. She waked at the fragrance of the god, which she smelled in the presence of his majesty. . . . When he came before her she rejoiced at the sight of his beauty, his love passed into her limbs, which the fragrance of the god flooded; all his odors were from Punt, the land of perfumes.

"He lay with her. And he said to her, 'Hatshepsut shall be the name of this my daughter, whom I have placed in thy body. She shall exercise the excellent kingship in this whole land.'

"There was more, much more. I shall relate that later. But what think you of this dream, my Overseer of the Fields? How do you interpret it? Is it a dream of moment, or one of small consequence, to be dismissed?"

All the while I speak, Senmut's eyes are on my face. He listens raptly, as though his whole being is absorbed by my tale. From time to time he nods.

There is an instant's silence, and then his words erupt like a gush of flame at a priestly ritual. "Your Highness, the dream is beautifully simple and clear. There can be only one explanation."

His eyes blaze and he falls again to his knees. On his face, before he bows to the floor, is an expression of . . . reverence.

I draw a breath. Clearly Senmut is convinced of the meaning of the dream. Perhaps more so than I. For to Senmut anything having to do with Amon or his wife, Mut, is evidently sacrosanct. And in my mind there remains a question. Somewhere, in the ancient accounts of long-dead theologians, is written that the old kings had been of truly divine birth. Has my dream merely evolved from that legend? Or, as I hope, comes it direct to me alone from the God of Gods?

"I thank you, Overseer," I say slowly. "Perhaps the tale will interest the First Prophet of Amon. But first I must have it firm in my heart."

"Your Majesty tells it well. I see and feel the scene as it is described."

He is well formed, this Senmut, eager but not rash, respectful but not obsequious, not yet so settled as a wheel into its own deep rut. His heart is open, like the clear glass of Syria, and in it I see my own thoughts mirrored. But enough.

I nod my dismissal. Senmut backs from the room. For a moment I muse on what other title would suit him: Controller of Works? Overseer of the Gardens of Amon? Later. Now I must prepare to face Hapusoneb with my dream.

Above all others, my Vizier's support is the most essential. I believe in my dream. Hapusoneb must believe in it also. Between the two of us I know we can persuade the whole of Egypt to believe—that my divine father Amon's wish is for his daughter Hatshepsut to reign, alone and all-powerful.

I push the unwieldy queen's crown of moon disc and horns higher on my forehead. The sun sears the bright canopy, flashing on the fluttering gold fringe till my head aches.

"You do not believe, Vizier, that the Prince will take an interest in domestic affairs?"

"Oh, I do not criticize, Majesty!"

No, Vizier never criticizes or complains—he is too wise. I trust him. Under my husband he was chancellor, and one of the few officials to take orders willingly from me whenever Thutmose was indisposed. Furthermore, we are related in a distant way: His father was one of the princes in my grandfather's court, born of a minor queen.

I smile at him. "I know that, Lord Hapusoneb. Come to me tomorrow. I desire your counsel on a matter."

"With pleasure, Majesty." He looks at me sadly. "Many difficulties would have been resolved, would never have emerged—forgive me my presumption—had your Highness been born of the other sex. Many of us feel that. But Majesty, blame such a bizarre statement on the summer heat and on a man longer in years than sense."

To that I make no reply, only wave him away.

That night the dream recurs, with further details. The God of Gods summons Khnum, the creator-god, and bids him model Amon's daughter, along with my *ka*, on his potter's wheel. Next I see my mother attended by Heket and three other traditional goddesses of birth and midwifery.

Myself, newly born, am held by my dear Hathor, goddess of love, and presented to Amon, who joyfully exclaims, "Welcome, my sweet daughter, my favorite, the King of Upper and Lower Egypt, the *maat* lover, Hatshepsut. Thou art king, taking possession of the Two Lands."

The more I ponder the dream, the clearer it becomes. Once and for all I am persuaded that thus it did happen: I was doubly fathered, as well by the God of Gods as by Great Pharaoh Thutmose I.

Still, despite these divine and powerful omens, I will be accused of fabricating the event. Possibly most of the men in Egypt will oppose me: my councillors, the court, the priesthood.

"For a queen to rule Egypt is unthinkable!" they will say. Very well. I will rule as a *king*. But first things first. Hapusoneb must have faith in my dream.

The following day, when I describe my dream to my Vizier, he appears stunned, even confused. Innately cautious, he is not so quick to grasp strange and unusual ideas as Senmut. But of course he is older and less pliable.

I am forced to repeat all facets of the dream two and often three times before Hapusoneb has it straight; it is like explaining something to a child. Nonetheless, since it is imperative to convince him, I very patiently describe once again Amon and the goddesses and my mother, the Great Queen Ahmose, and their words and their smiles and their joy, as they appeared in my dream. By now the particulars are as secure in my mind as my own face in a mirror.

"I believe this to be a divine sign, Vizier," I end, "a sign that Great God Amon wishes to rule—through me. That he wishes the temples of all the gods, especially his own, repaired and renewed throughout the length of Upper and Lower Egypt. He desires to make the land as strong internally as my father made it externally. And it *is* strong, it dominates the world. As you pointed out yesterday, the foreign vassals and their rich tribute are proof."

Vizier nods slowly. "Certainly . . . Egypt's dominance . . . is true." His expression is abstracted. He waits a minute or two, clears his throat before speaking further.

"Indeed, this appears to be a token direct from Amon, O Great Queen." His gaze, meeting mine, is not awed and no longer puzzled. It is hard to read, almost quizzical, almost . . . admiring.

What a surprising sort of man Hapusoneb is. No matter. He is First Prophet and Vizier, after Egypt's ruler the most powerful personage in the Two Lands. Like me, he has faith in divine and royal blood. And his words constitute a promise: *He will uphold me.*

In fact, he does a remarkable job of upholding, for he spreads word of my dream as efficiently as a farmer casts his grain for sowing. Many, many officials and noblemen approach me to express their wonder at

Amon's pronouncement. And perhaps, perceiving the design of things to come, to bid for my approval.

Senmut comes, too, every morning, to report on his duties. It is a pleasure to converse with him. Between his views, bold and innovative, and those of Hapusoneb, who is astute, experienced, more thoughtful, I draw a fine balance.

When I hint to Senmut that I lean toward grasping the reins of rulership with both hands rather than with only one, he speaks at once.

"But of course, Your Majesty! What else could you do, with Amon's message so clear?" He pauses an instant, then adds, "And once you are determined, should the act not take place quickly? There is little advantage in delay."

His opinion is the exact twin of the one in my head. How the auguries cluster, thick as a swarm of gnats, to sanction my decision!

I laugh. "Have you more advice to offer, Overseer?"

He considers, rubbing the back of his neck as he frequently does. . . . To promote thought? I wonder. The strap of his right sandal has rubbed a raw spot on the insole of his foot; he is, I suspect, a man who prefers going barefoot to being shod.

"Since you ask it, Great Queen . . ." He speaks with some reluctance.

"I do. I demand it."

"I hear things, Your Majesty. As Overseer of the Fields I have contact with many people in many places.

Know, then, that certain of the nobility favor the prospect of your rule. They fear further involvement with foreign places."

I nod.

"The First Prophet of Amon, Hapusoneb, supports you completely. But on the whole, the priesthood would prefer a warrior-pharaoh such as was your father. Foreign campaigns bring in booty to enrich Amon's temples, and conquest establishes Amon as foremost god in the world. The army, as is natural, prefers military expeditions to peace and in addition feels that Egypt's best defense is offense. Still . . . the army is much reduced from the time of your father and can hardly be counted a threat."

Seeing he has not finished, I break in. "Still more?"

He shrugs ruefully. "A few dream of Egypt's endless expansion. And there are always some deeply disapproving of a queen-pharaoh."

"You tell me then that I have enemies?"

"Enemies. Better said . . . friends of the young Prince."

Abruptly my whole being fills with rage as a cup fills to overflowing with wine. "Fools! Do they believe I aim to depose him? He has not yet the years to reign. He will have his turn. No land can be well governed by two rulers at once. They serve to divide, not unite, the people."

Far from being shaken by my anger, Senmut surveys me calmly.

My voice is harsh. "So what do you counsel, Overseer?"

"I would suggest, Your Majesty, that you make certain of every member of your council. You will need a loyal government to offset the priesthood."

"I intend to do so. Leave me now."

I pace back and forth to cool my fury—or my guilt. Senmut speaks truly. It goes without saying I will face opposition. The step I contemplate taking is serious, hazardous even. Queen-rulers of Egypt (there have been two or three, all many years ago) have ever been considered a disaster for the country. But I will show them differently. I can be as worthy a monarch as any in history.

Why should the priesthood defy me? They serve Amon as I serve him, faithfully and with deep reverence. I propose to honor his name throughout the Black Land with fine shrines and temples. Yet . . . Senmut is right. The priesthood will resist me, if only because I am a woman. Well, I will show them—by being such a woman as they have never seen.

As to my council . . . I mull over their names. Hapusoneb, yes. Chief Treasurer Kenut, decidedly not. He opposes me, and in a careless manner as though I were a fly to be brushed away. He will learn to his detriment that a woman's vanity is not lightly to be bruised.

Chancellor Nuni? Hmmmm. He vacillates, tasting

of two dishes at once. I will "promote" him to Royal Sandal Bearer or some such innocuous title while I appoint Thuty, cousin and friend, as Chancellor.

Lord Ineni will remain as Chief Architect to the King, and Min-Nekhet, Father's old soldier companion, will become Chief of Works. The young Puyemre, whom I named as Second Priest of Amon, is working out well. He oversees the work executed by the temple artists and craftsmen and has produced some outstanding sculptors and cabinetmakers. Besides, his laugh is infectious; the council can stand some humor.

Other offices I must give more thought to: Chief Steward, Overseer of the Granaries, Commander in Chief of the Army among them. Above all they must be filled by men loyal to me. One could be held by Senmut.

No. He is too important to assign a static role, like that of the red and black men in the game *senet*. He must be left as free as the ivory wand that prescribes the play. Oh, Senmut, I have plans for you.

A short scene takes place between my stepson and me. It is my duty to inform him of the step I am taking, and I do so.

"At present thou art too young to rule. So I will assume that task myself. Thou wilt not have to shoulder such heavy responsibilities for some years yet."

As usual Thutmose stands with bowed head, studying the floor. Its pattern seems to interest him far more than my words.

I pause, wondering if my divine dream would have

meaning for him. I decide not; one of the Prince's feet is carefully following a design in the tile. Quite possibly he has not heard any of my explanation.

"Dost thou understand, my son?" My voice is sharper than I had intended.

He nods dutifully. "Yes, gracious Majesty."

I sigh and dismiss him. Not once during the interview has he raised his eyes to mine.

CHAPTER 7

And so arrangements for my coronation go forward. The sooner it takes place, the better. For plots of defiance to hatch, time is essential. We will dispense with time.

Throughout the Two Lands and abroad, the edict of my ascension to the throne is sent, only a few weeks before the ceremony. By tradition the event takes place on a major religious holiday, in this case the Feast of Opet. Hapusoneb insists this is a bit hurried but perfectly proper. But then anything Pharaoh-to-be decides is proper.

The edict reads:

A letter of the King to cause thee to know that My Majesty is risen as King on the throne of Horus, without equal forever. My titles are: for my Horus name,

Usert-Kau, mighty in kas; *for Vulture-Cobra, Uadjit-Renpet, fresh in years; for Golden Horus, Netert-khau, divine in apparitions; my royal and birth names, Makare Hatshepsut.*

Cause thou that worship of the gods be made at the desire of the King of Upper and Lower Egypt, Hatshepsut. Cause thou that all oaths be taken in the name of My Majesty, born of the royal mother Ahmose. This is written that thou mayest bow thy head in obedience and knowest that the royal house is firm and strong.

The third year, third month of Inundation, day 7. Day of Coronation.

I worry over my dress. As ceremony demands that the king wear the royal braided beard strapped to his chin (no matter whether he has a beard of his own or not), I shall certainly do so. Ought I, then, to wear the long dress of a queen or the short kilt of a king? With a question Hapusoneb supplies the answer.

He is preoccupied, poor man, at having to oversee so many elaborate arrangements in such a short period of time. At each succeeding audience with me he appears more harried, more bent with care, until his back curves like a strung bow.

"One of the problems, Majesty, is that the titles and coronation ceremonies are designed for men. How are we to change them?"

The solution strikes me, clear as Hapusoneb's harassed face.

"There is no need to change anything, Vizier. I mean to rule as a king, with the full powers of a king. And I shall dress as a king. The rituals, the titles, will remain the same as those initiated by Narmer, first King of the Two Lands."

Hapusoneb appears dubious, then relieved. After all, he can scarcely overrule Pharaoh-to-be, no matter what his misgivings.

And as I am resolved to be as resolute, as forceful as any king, I will begin by donning full regalia for my coronation. Around my waist, over the short kilt, I fasten a broad belt adorned with a metal buckle in the form of my personal cartouche. Tied to it in front is an apron of beads, in back a bull's tail. A girl attaches the beard to my chin. Over my wig is fitted the *nems*, the leather headcloth with the two striped lappets falling forward over my shoulders.

For the ceremony I have ordered a dazzling gold-and-jeweled pectoral suspended from a double gold chain. On each of my arms a girl clasps a pair of wide bracelets, another on each wrist, a third pair on my ankles. On my fingers rings are strung like chunks of beef on skewers. Surely I must weigh twice as much as usual.

As I take a final peek in my silver mirror, I gasp to Henut, "But I look a mummy! One can hardly see the flesh for the gold."

"Very appropriate, Highness." Henut nods approvingly. "Egypt is wealthy beyond measure. You are the symbol of that wealth."

Perhaps so, but wealth, I find, does not always signal comfort.

The ceremony goes off with fanfare. Although the coronation of my husband occurred fifteen years before, the rites are still clear in my memory.

I sit on a light throne borne by six slaves from the Great House to the royal barge, which carries us down the river. From the shore to the temple the procession is headed by heralds crying, "Earth, beware! Your god comes!" Rows of soldiers pace before and behind my carrying chair, and in back of them hundreds of priests.

Behind my chair a servant supports a long-handled sunshade to provide me some relief from the sun, and beside me two young pages wave fans of ostrich plumes. (Vizier has promised boys with endurance and dedication enough not to whack off my headpiece.) The tail of the procession—a very long tail—is made up of government dignitaries, the nobility, and foreign envoys.

Most of the spectators sink to their knees, heads in the dust, although a few bewildered country folk stand gaping in amazement. A guard motions them sternly to bow, or even strikes one or two with his spear. As Hapusoneb says, "Manners grow more and more out of fashion." Still, the atmosphere is a happy mixture of reverence and rejoicing.

In the main hall of the temple my litter is lowered and I walk, accompanied by the High Priest, to the gleaming gilded throne set on a dais. After prayers and hymns to Amon, the Priest makes an address in which he repeats my father's words uttered in the dream: "I have appointed her to be my successor upon my throne. She it is, assuredly, who shall sit upon my glorious throne; she shall order all matters for the people in every department of the state; she it is who shall lead you."

Finally he pronounces me Lord of the Two Lands, seated on the Horus-throne, and living forever and ever. Into my hands he puts the two scepters, emblems of Osiris: the golden crook, and the golden flail with its handle carved in the form of a lotus flower. And on my head he places one symbolic crown after another, ending with the double crown, combining the white crown of Upper Egypt and the red of Lower Egypt, with the golden uraeus, or cobra, attached to the front. The cobra has the reputation of spitting poisonous fire at anyone venturing too near to Pharaoh. (Someday for amusement I must persuade Vizier to test this.) The whole contraption is so heavy that my neck soon aches with the weight.

During the crowning I notice my daughter and the Prince standing beside each other. As Nefrure refused to ride in a carrying chair for fear of falling, the two march (when Nefrure is not being carried by a guard) in the procession, close behind my litter. Nefrure beams at me, proud and excited, while Thutmose's gaze is as blank as when he viewed the gems and vases at the reception of ambassadors. Lost in his own world (perhaps a world where his stepmother is either feeble or dead), he seems oblivious of all movement about him.

The return journey to the palace is agonizing, so that I have to grit my teeth and lock my neck in position. What if suddenly my neck were to bend— or break—and the unwieldy crown bounce off onto the pavement and into the crowd? King Hatshepsut would have to fabricate a glib story; else all of Egypt would believe that Amon had sent a warning that I was unfit to be Pharaoh. I shudder and lock my neck even more tightly.

Finally it is over. I am home in my suite, resting, my head and neck painful but still intact. The reception and banquet lie ahead, but those I can manage easily. In the distance I hear the celebration of the people, with their eating and drinking, their singing and dancing, their roars of amusement at the acrobats and jugglers and clowns provided for their entertainment. Egypt's treasury will sink this day like the Nile during harvest, but then coronations do not happen every day, that of a queen practically never.

I, Makare Hatshepsut, am Pharaoh of all of Egypt! The thought is too stupendous to fit into my head just yet. First I must view it from all sides . . . and stroke it . . . and shape it . . . till it can slip naturally into place.

An attendant announces Senmut. I had requested him to mingle with the crowd, listen to reactions, report to me his findings.

"Majesty, they are happy. The good inundation this year helps to set their mood. The bountiful food and drink provided today by the state complete the setting.

A few, spying the beard, have not yet realized Your Majesty is a queen. The others accept the fact."

He is a kind man. If there are grumblings he will not spoil my day with them.

"Lord Senmut," I say impulsively, "My Majesty confers on you as of now the rank of nobility and the title of Unique Friend. As well as the office of Conductor of Festivals. Efficiency and loyalty will never go unrewarded in my court."

He smiles—a rare and charming smile. I feel a quick regret that he was not born a prince.

His words interrupt my thought. "One question troubles everyone, Your Majesty."

"And that is?" I ask, surprised.

"How is Your Majesty to be addressed? As 'Her Majesty' or 'His Majesty,' as 'Queen Hatshepsut' or 'King Hatshepsut'?"

From anyone else I should consider the question impertinent. From Senmut it is candid and direct and amusing. And quite proper, really. I envision the Vizier, tangled in a snarl of protocol, attempting to discover a reasonable solution to the question.

And after, if I do not care for his solution, I will announce my own decision. And that will be that.

PART 3
PHARAOH

CHAPTER 8

Year 3 of the Reign
of His Majesty Makare Hatshepsut

"Day 14, month 3 of Sowing . . ." While only three months have passed since my coronation, I date my reign as beginning from the death of my husband. It gives a more settled appearance. And in truth I did begin my rule then, for what use was the presence of a nine-year-old boy?

I, Makare Hatshepsut, am Pharaoh of the whole of Egypt, with no fetters, no restraints to hinder me. I know now how a caged bird feels when at long last the door flaps open and it can escape into the limitless blue of heaven.

It is not that I desire power for its own sake. I am not so vainglorious. But to have the authority to do what I know must be done for my country's good— that is ecstasy. Also—to be completely truthful—I desire to demonstrate to Egypt, to the entire world, that a woman can rule every bit as wisely as a man.

Each morning when Henut wakes me, I lie for a moment not thinking at all, only savoring this enormous bubble of happiness. Arching my neck over the cushioned headrest, I watch a sliver of sunlight enter the high window and light up the curly frieze border of the ceiling. The chariot of Amon begins its journey across the clear sky just as I am about to begin *my* day.

For another moment I ponder my goals as ruler. I will make Egypt stronger than she has ever been—so strong internally that no country will ever dare challenge her.

I will repair all the temples in the land, in particular those which the vagabond Hyksos neglected for so long. In addition, I will construct others to be the most beautiful in the world.

And—an idea lodged in a far corner of my mind— I may in time launch a sailing expedition to Punt, that faraway place we know as God's Land, the source of our indispensable frankincense and myrrh. This can in name be a trading expedition, but in fact a purpose just as important will be to explore, to observe the wonders of the Great Green, of the manners and customs of the Puntites, of the nature of their land. I may command that expedition myself. For I am immensely inquisitive about foreign peoples, how they live and dress and think. Curiosity may be a queenly rather than kingly trait, but in any case, I intend to indulge it.

"It is the hour, Highness."

Henut stands beside my bed, a fresh linen robe in her hands. I slip into the robe, into my sandals. Henut runs a comb through my hair, adjusts a heavy, elaborate wig. I am ready for the first ritual of the morning.

Outside the door wait two high priestesses of Amon, one wearing the mask of Horus, the other the ibis head of Thoth. They bow. We walk in silence down the hall to the House of the Morning, my main chapel.

Inside, the golden ewers of water stand ready on a marble-topped table. Removing my robe, I lave my body, speaking aloud a prayer.

"Great Father God Amon-Re, as thou bathest in the ocean each morning to begin thy journey across the heavens, so bathes thy daughter. Thus we restore our divine vitality for the day's tasks. Guide me, O my father, to live in *maat* for today and always."

The priestesses anointing me, helping to robe me, are a symbol of triumph. They are the result of my first victory as ruler over Amon's priesthood.

The day I ascended the throne, a chief priest informed me, "Each morning two priestesses will accompany Her Majesty to the House of the Morning. As Her Majesty may know, a king is attended by priests wearing the masks of Horus and Thoth. This would of course be unsuitable in the case of Her Majesty." His voice held an edge of superiority.

"Perhaps my proclamation has not reached your ears, Lord," I replied icily. "My Majesty, being king, is referred to by the whole world as *His* Majesty.

Furthermore, the priestesses will naturally don the masks of Horus and Thoth."

Shock and indignation so overcame him that he stammered. "S-such a custom is unheard of in the en-entire h-history of the Two Lands!" He glared at me, suddenly realized who—or what—I was, and gulped.

"I beg Her . . . His Majesty's pardon, but for women . . . priestesses to wear the sacred masks defies the holy tradition of Amon's ritual."

"Then we will change tradition. See that the female Thoth and Horus await My Majesty tomorrow." I dismissed him brusquely. He stumbled away, his face pale even for a priest.

They resent me, the priests, and will yet cause me trouble—I sense it. Despite all I do for Amon. However, for the time all goes well. With use customs come quickly to be accepted, and after three months the priestesses and their masks have become routine.

After my ablutions we proceed to another chapel, already occupied by priests and court officials. Here more prayers are said, and a high priest intones, "May a curse be laid, O Amon, on anyone who offends thee, with or without intention."

Later the same priest feels called on to reassure me. "The curse is aimed at His Majesty's ministers, certainly not at His Majesty himself." But swiftly adds, "His Majesty takes note, I am sure, of all prayers as a guide to royal conduct."

His tone reminds me of Tutami in the classroom: condescending patronage. At times—many times—

the priesthood takes on the all-powerful airs of Amon. It could do with a lesson in humility.

Sacrifice and the reading of the entrails follow: A priest spells out the omens. The day is auspicious for the composing of letters, for the holding of audience, for the visiting of friends. Inauspicious for journeys, either by boat or palanquin or foot. (That I could have forecast myself. There is enough work to keep me occupied at home for some time.)

At last I am escorted back to my quarters. After perfuming my mouth with wine and fruit, I submit to being readied, not so tedious a process as it was when I was a child. For one thing, there is no Pekey to yank my hair or skin my flesh. She has long since vanished from the palace, probably to ply her skill in some noblewoman's home. For another thing, it is a quiet time to think and plan.

Were I a man, I could confer with my officials while being groomed. However, most of my council would die of embarrassment if called on to witness the plucking of my brows, the massage with unguents, the application of kohl and henna. As a dozen corpses would be of no help to me, I think alone.

One problem is that of Prince Thutmose. How he views my dream of divine birth I do not know. Nor do I care. Deep in my mind this lack of interest concerning Thutmose bothers me. Thorough and careful always in my planning, I do not forget the obstacles, however small, which like sharp stones protrude through the path of my life.

The Prince is such an obstacle. He is more than a stone. Rather, he is a vein of rock that appears treacherously now here, now there, for me to stumble over. One day he may loom before me, a high jagged barrier.

Well. The rock lies there, I am aware of it, and there is nothing to do about it. For the time being.

Yesterday Hapusoneb made a suggestion: Why did I not place the Prince under his care as apprentice priest? It is an honor due a prince to serve the Great God of No-Amon. There he would be under the eye of the entire priesthood.

Under *your* eye, O Hapusoneb, perhaps. The entire priesthood may not be so trustworthy. At all events, the idea has merit and I shall consider it.

While my hair is being dressed, I glance over accounts of palace expenditures. To think I once complained (to be truthful not once but many times) of having to learn to read. How thoughtless children are. True it is they do not know what is good for them.

The palace expenses are revealing. So much waste. No doubt kings seldom pay heed to such petty details, but this is a field I can understand and correct. Not only disbursements of the Great House but those made throughout the government can and shall be curtailed. Some officials act as though the lotuses of the Nile were of gold and have only to be plucked. They shall learn.

As an example, I have cut my immediate toilet staff to twenty. My husband had twice that number, including four barbers to shave him when he surely had beard enough for one alone.

I have limited my attendants to one mat spreader, two manicurists and two pedicurists (all four work at once to save time), three hairdressers, two masseuses, four perfumers (well, one to daub on scent and three others to distill the oils and mix the fragrances), one to prepare my bath, two to dress me, two to apply cosmetics, one to adjust my jewelry (my mother used three such, but to her all jewels were lucky or unlucky depending on the day, and this had to be determined by divination). I do not count laundresses, bleachers, pressers, seamstresses.

Today, with one public appearance, and that an informal one, I will dress as a woman. That means a gown instead of a kilt, a light wig, and crown. What an advantage I have over other pharaohs. I can choose my sex as it pleases me.

A whisper. "Majesty?"

The Keeper of Royal Jewelry stands before me, a tray of gold collars in her hands. They are too heavy, appropriate for formal functions. I shake my head and wave her away to fetch other, lighter necklets.

She returns with a necklace of thin gold wires woven about delicate flowers of pearls and amethysts. And with it my favorite earrings, those the Great God Pharaoh, my father, presented me when I was nine. They are butterflies, their wings of lapis lazuli and garnet, fastened to gold loops. I nod. Why cannot one's officials be as eager and amenable as servants?

A discreet cough disturbs my musing. "Your Majesty."

Only Henut dares interrupt my thoughts. I glance up.

My twenty attendants stand in stiff rows like soldiers, their gaze on the floor. Henut stands before them, her eyes plucking their stance, their hands, their expression, as she would pluck feathers from a goose. If any is found wanting, that one will know shortly.

It appears I am readied for the day.

First is scheduled a conference with Chief Treasurer Nehesi. Nehesi is the newest of my councillors, unearthed by Hapusoneb, my faithful minister of a myriad connections.

The Treasurer is a small man, as shriveled as a dried fig. Son of a Nubian brewer, he completely lacks the elegance and assurance of the average courtier. Far more important, he knows and understands value.

For years he was a middleman at the market, dealing in that unit of commerce called the *shat*. Father once explained to me the meaning of the word:

"As an example, my daughter, let us take the seller of a cow. In exchange for it, he is offered so many bushels of corn or lengths of linen or jars of wine. But, being fond of his cow, he decides the animal is worth more than what is offered. The difference then must be calculated in so many *shat*, and an item of that worth agreed on."

"I should not at all mind doing such work," I told

him. "To aid seller and purchaser to find articles of equal value—it is a kind of game."

Father chuckled (I was the cause of many of his smiles and laughs). "A kind of game, yes. Didst thou know, Hatshepsut, that some countries base their unit of value on metal, copper or silver or gold?"

I put my nose in the air. "That would be a clumsy system, metal being so heavy and cumbersome."

Father nodded. "A practice to be expected of foreign lands."

Well, what else? In its ideas and practices my Egypt is years in advance of other nations.

Father would have approved of Nehesi: his careful honesty, his tenacity, his precision, his refusal to be intimidated . . . except by *me*. My Treasurer has yet to figure me out and tends to handle me as gingerly as he would an ostrich egg.

Our conference goes well—better for me than for him. After the usual review of revenue and disbursement, he hesitantly broaches a new subject.

"Your Majesty, the Chief Steward brings to my attention"—he pauses, coughs nervously—"a trivial matter. Of very minor importance." He stops again, struggles to heave up the words he wants. He takes a deep breath, and lo, the words come gushing forth. "Your Majesty, there are complaints from the royal household regarding the inadequate ration of bread." He bows his head. (For me to strike it off?)

I allow my arched brows to arch higher. "How is

99

this possible? Do we not provide fourteen hundred loaves a day?"

"Indeed, your Majesty. Oh, indeed. His Majesty may be unaware that Great God-King Thutmose made provision for *two thousand* loaves daily."

"Treasurer, my staff is much reduced from that era. There is now no harem, and fewer personal attendants."

"True, true. But . . . to maintain His Majesty's residence in the appropriate style for a monarch of His Majesty's glorious status, an adequate household staff is absolutely necessary. The staff has grown, of necessity with His Majesty's tremendous responsibilities, to a somewhat greater size than that of the Great God-King Thutmose II. . . ."

Here he marks my frown at mention of my husband's name and leaps to a happier note. "His Majesty will be most gratified to learn that—this from a memorandum of the Chief Steward—the palace has decreased the amount of beer consumed from 200 to 150 jugs a day. Except, of course, when the amount is augmented for holidays."

Which means ten days out of thirty. My subjects live for feast days.

"My Majesty is well pleased about the beer. But back to the bread. My Majesty detests waste and will not provide for gorging."

The Treasurer is unused to women who argue and is thrown off balance. "Your Highness, could we . . . if I may . . . Your Majesty, with the addition of two hundred loaves more, I believe there would be no waste. And no further complaints."

I ponder. An idea sprouts, leafs out, flowers. It is a good idea and has additional merit: It will flick the priesthood's too-haughty nose.

"Lord Nehesi, the state is making major repairs and improvements on Amon's temple. My Majesty has in mind rich gifts, additions to the temple such as statues, obelisks, fine new ceremonial robes for the priests. In return for these, we will request the temple to supply the Great House with two hundred loaves of bread daily."

My Treasurer smiles thinly. Still overawed by a female sovereign, he cannot believe I am serious in demanding bread from Amon's domain. On discovering that I mean what I say, he wonders if the temple will blame *him* for the proposal, which could have uncomfortable effects; the priesthood can be vindictive in subtle ways.

I have faith in Nehesi's astuteness. Blame can be shared by the Chief Steward, by a dozen other officials. At any rate, I have solved that problem with no increase in my budget. My people will not say of me, "Ah! She flings gold dust about as though it were sand."

Actually Egypt's finances are at present in excellent shape. Our hundreds of granaries in temples and towns are well stocked in the event of a light inundation and the resulting failure of crops. The construction of private buildings is brisk, bringing in good revenue from the state monopoly in brick making; the same is true in papermaking. Fortunately for me, taxation on harvests and ships and property need not be increased this year.

A thought occurs: With my head so full of economies, large and small, I could always find occupation as a simple housewife!

CHAPTER 9

Next on my schedule, I show myself for the first time as Pharaoh at the Window of Appearances. My excuse to the Vizier is that the people adore spectacles of any sort, and a view of Pharaoh is regarded as a grand treat. To be quite honest, I do it for pure pleasure. To distribute largesse in my own name, with no one to nod me permission—ah, I relish that.

Always before, I had stood behind my father or my husband and was handed a small bracelet or two to toss. Today Nefrure alone appears with me. She bounces with anticipation.

"Calm thyself," I chide her.

"Oh, my mother, I do not like to be calm!"

She peers over the railing at the courtyard. It being a hot and windless day, the court is packed with sun-shade bearers and fan bearers as well as household officials and relatives of the honorees. A guard marshals the recipients into a queue. On three sides the public, wiping their perspiring faces, strain against the ropes. Even the lowliest wears a clean loincloth for the occasion.

There are seven or eight honorees. As each steps before the balcony and salutes me, I deliver a short speech of praise, ending with "Thou art my faithful servant who hast carried out the orders of My Majesty, who is well pleased with thee. I therefore award thee these gifts with the words 'Thou shalt eat the bread of Pharaoh (Life, Health, Strength!) thy lord, in the temple of Amon.' "

From the tray of gold ornaments I choose necklets, rings, inlaid hatchets, goblets, trinkets in the shapes of bees and lions, to fling to those honored. As the gifts are caught, there are shrieks of delight from the family.

Nefrure is in raptures. She helps to shower "the praise of gold" on her friends Hapusoneb (honored for faithful and meritorious service) and Senmut (for outstanding ideas concerning efficiency and economies in government departments). They will need to grow new necks to wear all the chains she flings to them.

"Senmut needs another bracelet!" Nefrure exclaims, eyes bright with excitement. As I have appointed him her tutor, she sees much of him. They have grown very fond of each other.

"He will not be able to wear so much jewelry or

carry it either," I protest. "There will be other opportunities."

"Tomorrow?" she asks hopefully.

I laugh. "Not tomorrow, but very soon."

The last award goes to the Keeper of the Interior Apartments for long and industrious service. "Meritorious" and "outstanding" can certainly not be applied to him, nor, I fear, can "faithful." The ceremony will reduce the sting when tomorrow I replace him in office. He is a relic of my husband's rule, disapproves vocally of queen rulers, and treats with no merchant or servant without a fat bribe. His wife is as oily as he, her eyes as shifty as his as she peeps into my face, incredulous that a mere *woman* is capable of filling the throne of the Two Lands. Stupid creature! Ah well, after today I will see little of them. He will be offered the position of Messenger for the Dogs' Food, which he is not likely to accept.

After lunch I escape to my refuge, a chamber furnished with only a long sofa and a small table to hold refreshments. With no other clutter, I can imagine I am on my country estate, the tiles of the floor tinted green as grass, the ceiling molded and painted to resemble a grape arbor, the vines thick with purple fruit.

Here I admit only Henut, to massage my forehead for headache, and my daughter (during those rare moments when she agrees to act like a lady). Today I have invited Senmut—Lord Senmut, as he has been for a month.

Senmut. Ah, Hatshepsut, in spite of thy royal and

divine blood and against thy strongest wishes, thou art proved to be all too mortal. To hear the name of Senmut, to glimpse Senmut, to hear Senmut's voice— my breath, my blood cease in their courses, my vision clouds, my ears ring, my head is light.

What does it mean? Surely not that I love him. I have never loved anyone—apart from my dear Egypt— besides my father, and my daughter. I do not allow myself to love anyone. I cannot afford to. Love is weakness. I tell myself that over and over: Love is weakness. Only . . . how do I control my blood, my breath?

I question myself severely. Why do I find this man appealing? He is not handsome, although his face is unique, the features clear cut like his character, mouth thin, eyes both wide and long. The nose is somewhat hooked but not, thanks be to Hathor, as prominent as my own family's nose. The mobility of expression constitutes its charm.

His most significant traits are his boldness of out-look, his self-assurance, his adaptibility. As my daughter's tutor he has proved his gentleness, for she can tax one's patience with her teasing.

I say that he is adaptable; already he has adopted the dress, the manners, the carriage, the viewpoint of a nobleman. No. In all frankness he has not done so completely.

With regard to the gods, I have noticed, he is un-sophisticated and highly superstitious. And he pos-sesses a peasant's unabashed urge for acquisition. The offices I appoint him to he fulfills without fault. But the titles of those offices he collects and wears as a rustic woman flaunts at one time every string of cheap beads she owns. On all letters, all proclamations, Senmut never fails to include each and every title. Still, modesty is by no means a national characteristic of ours.

Today I confer with Senmut in his new capacity as Controller of Works. We will discuss the reopening of our copper and turquoise mines in the Sinai. (My composure is flawless. No blush, no tremble, no shortness of breath is apparent.)

"The reworking of the mines," I explain, "will require the presence of troops to ensure security from the barbaric sand dwellers. Aside from protection, the project will serve to keep the men occupied. The officers tend to become quickly restless unless they are busy warring and conquering."

Having been at one time a military scribe, Senmut is aware of how the military mind works. He nods.

"The plan is good. The officers will welcome it more than their men."

I look at him inquiringly.

"The common soldiers dislike setting foot on foreign soil. They ask, 'What if we die there? Who will prepare our bodies for burial? Who will recite the ritual over us? Are we to lose eternity because we leave our beloved Egypt?' I fear you must count on some desertions."

An idea comes to mind. These days find me as full

of ideas as a palm tree with dates. I make haste to pluck the ideas and put them to work before they rot on the branches. "I will see that a body of priests and two or three embalmers accompany the men. That should allay their fear."

And if I follow Hapusoneb's suggestion of placing the Prince under his supervision as an apprentice priest—which appears most reasonable—then in two or three years' time the boy can himself become part of such an expedition to Sinai. It will provide him training and experience. And it will remove him effectively from the scene of action—for a time.

"That will cheer the men." Senmut's tone approves my decision.

"Have you yourself lived away from Egypt?" I ask.

"At one time. I built a grain warehouse and later the courthouse for the colony that Great Pharaoh Thutmose II"—he bows his head—"established in Cush."

"You engineered those buildings?"

He grimaces slightly. "They were nothing. But seeing them, the general Huy requested me to construct a house in the country for his newly married daughter. *That* I was proud of."

"So you are an architect." Is there no end to this man's talents? "Have you constructed other edifices?"

"A new home for my parents. My tomb and theirs. The deepest joy of life comes from creating a structure—a cottage, a mansion, a palace."

"In which of these did you grow up?"

"The first, Your Majesty. My father is a farmer, and his farm is very small."

"Then you have done doubly well." I contemplate another idea. With deliberation I ask, "Have you ever dreamed of designing a temple? A mortuary temple?"

Senmut draws in a deep breath, holds it for a full minute. His eyes, fixed on my feet, have turned to glass.

The breath pours out in a sigh, and his eyes meet mine. "A dream far beyond hope. Does His Majesty have such a temple in mind?"

Lord Senmut wastes no time in circling a subject. He even takes away *my* breath.

"The place for a temple, yes," I say slowly. "The shape of the temple itself, no." I change my tone to one of indifference. "Should you be interested, you might submit a plan."

He is at once all business. "Indeed, Majesty, I am interested. Would you tell me the site of this temple?"

"Near the tomb of Great Pharaoh Mentuhotep, built some six hundred years ago. As you are aware, it lies close to the valley where my own father is buried."

"It is a magnificent setting. Oh yes. Precisely right for a temple." Already his mind is churning, his eyes bright, his face flushed with the challenge.

To my chagrin I find myself jealous of this challenge. Would his face liven, his eyes glow so fervently if he thought of me as "Hatshepsut" rather than as "His Majesty"? Or—terrible thought—does he use me only to further his ambition? Ah, what a tangle is life! The lowly alone can afford to be direct. I dismiss Lord Senmut with a cool smile.

One further task remains to be done this day. During a short visit to the temple of Amon to view the alterations, I have an interview with my stepson, who has his lessons there. He is not a likable boy. The royal blood in him is so weakened by the common fluid of his mother that he is little better than a peasant. And looks it. Even for eleven years he is thin and knobby. How Egypt would fare under his rule I tremble to think. We will put it off as long as possible. Perhaps forever.

The Third Priest of Amon, Lord Rensonb, is also present. He is a lean, cold, unyielding man with a head like a skull, a fanatic fervor for detail, and a sensitive stomach. According to Hapusoneb, his moods match the state of this organ, which is generally sour.

The story goes that upon learning that I was to ascend the throne, he threw himself on the temple floor before the shrine of Amon and declared that he would die there of starvation rather than see a woman as king. His miserable stomach saved his life; its protest at being denied sustenance was more than he could bear. However, instead of blaming his stomach for his failure, he blamed me.

I nod to Rensonb and address the Prince. "My Majesty has decided to place thee in the Great Temple in order to serve Amon. Would this please thee?"

I sound pompous without meaning to. The boy

makes me uncomfortable, he is always so silent and noncommittal.

"I thank thee, yes, gracious Majesty." His voice is shrill, the words are sedate, his glance never lifts from the floor.

"Good. The lord Hapusoneb will oversee thy duties."

He bows, saying nothing.

I turn to the Third Priest.

"Then, Lord, My Majesty leaves the Prince in your hands in the hope he will do honor to the God of Gods."

Never one for humility, the Third Priest must have his say. "His Majesty may rest assured. As the future ruler of the Two Lands, the Prince will be given the best of training."

"For that reason My Majesty places him here." My tone is curt.

"The best of training. And the most intensive. Within three or four years the Prince will be prepared to take his place as king."

I am floored by his presumption. My temper, as uncontrollable as Rensonb's stomach, boils up.

"*When* he becomes king is no concern of yours, Lord Rensonb. As director of the temple school you will superintend his education. From First Prophet Hapusoneb My Majesty will receive reports of the Prince's progress—and of *your* efficiency as educator."

I turn my back on him, nod farewell to Thutmose.

For once the boy's face is less impassive than a toad's. The exchange of words has actually upset him; his mouth is wide open as he bows.

It has upset me, also. Were the Third Priest any other man, I would replace him immediately, expel him to some small temple in Cush. But Rensonb's family is as old as my own and was at one time as noble. The manner of ridding myself of him must be subtle. Meanwhile, under Hapusoneb's eye he will hesitate to plant seditious ideas in my stepson's head— I trust.

My conversation with Senmut comes to mind, and a vague scheme grows strong. Very well, little son. Within the year thou wilt journey to the Sinai—well away from Rensonb and from thy mother, Isis—where thy stamina and character will be tested. The desert is an oven and abounds in snakes and poisonous insects, wild and wily tribesmen who resent intrusion. If thou weatherest all these, young Prince, thou mayest acquire worthy blood on thy own. In time—years and years from now—thou mayest even succeed me. *If* no one more suitable appears.

Back at the palace, a scroll is handed me, and my dejection vanishes. It is a sketch, very rough, of Senmut's design for my temple. He has taken the plan of Mentuhotep's shrine but enlarged and improved on it. The longer I study it, the more I feel it can be worked into a superb model. Mine will be the most beautiful temple, the most magnificent building in all the Two Lands! And justly so, for I wish to be remembered always as a queen who became a king . . . a king greatest of the great.

The location is a kind of amphitheater, and the backdrop of my temple consists of high, rugged, towering cliffs. Instead of a tall, imposing structure that would be lost against the steep cliffs, Senmut has drawn a low but extremely wide building. There are three ascending terraces, like gigantic steps, connected by ramps. Each terrace consists of a huge courtyard leading into a colonnaded hall, the roof of each hall forming the courtyard of the hall above. The complex will be immense; we Egyptians build big, as we think big.

The glory of the plan is in its contrast to the background and in its simplicity. Even the terraces resemble my vision of the myrrh terraces of Punt, the original garden of the gods.

I am too excited by the plan to think. Originally I had thought to require plans from a half dozen of No-Amon's finest architects. Now there is no need. No one in the entire world or in the next thousand years could conceive a design so exactly right. Had I been an artist, I should myself have designed a temple just so. Of course it is still a sketch only, a bare outline—but oh, it has promise.

Tomorrow I will announce my acceptance of the plan to the Great Ones, my council, and give orders to begin work as soon as possible. The embellishment of halls and courtyards can be worked out later. The matter itself is settled.

This means, too, that I will see much of Lord Senmut. Hatshepsut, reel in thy heart before it dies of throbbing! So be it. As I rise, so Senmut shall rise.

He is vital, dynamic . . . almost an extension of myself. I even feel he understands me—which certainly no one else living does. With all my wariness and distrust, I do not mind this. Even a pharaoh needs someone to understand him. But only *one* someone, no more. And this someone I will make to love me. Truly love me.

"Hathor, dear goddess of love, I will have Senmut build thee an altar!" I whisper. "Thanks upon thanks I send thee. Thou hast blessed me with someone to love. . . . I will have the most splendid temple in Egypt. . . . The boy's future is decided. . . . Above all, I am King of the Two Lands! No, Hathor, thou deservest more than an altar. I will build thee a chapel within my very own temple!"

Even for a pharaoh, joy does not endure. But this day I will forever remember as joyful.

CHAPTER 10

Year 4 of the Reign
of His Majesty Makare Hatshepsut

A year has passed since my decision to send Thutmose to the Sinai. He is now old enough to endure the journey and the work itself. In his way he will be making history, for my policy includes the opening or reworking of the copper, gold, and turquoise mines in the eastern deserts, thus providing Upper and Lower Egypt with new sources of wealth. This should help satisfy the priesthood's greed for gold.

As one of several priests, the Prince will minister to the laborers who work the copper mines and the soldiers sent to protect them. It will be a relief to have him gone. His presence serves to remind the priesthood of their resentment of a woman king.

My reasons for my stepson's assignment are practical: The Prince is to uphold the honor of Amon abroad, to see something of the world, to serve in a useful capacity rather than as an ornament. Thutmose himself agrees with me.

When I propose to him that he accompany the group to the mines, his eyes brighten and for once his self-possession disappears.

"It is a splendid idea, Majesty! There will be chance for adventure—I hope. The sand dwellers may attack us; the desert tribes are fierce, I believe. I shall practice shooting and spear throwing so as to be well prepared."

Never have I seen him exhibit such ardor, never have I heard such a spate of words from him. My stepson glows with pleasure as though I have done him the most remarkable favor. Well yes. Were I a boy of twelve, I, too, should jump for joy at this opportunity.

My Council of Government offers little resistance, although at first it is lukewarm in approval. When I broach the subject, there are skeptical faces, clearing of uncertain throats, and pursing of lips. But enthusiasm, I find, is a great antidote to doubts. After I point out the advantages to Thutmose in the appointment (of those to myself I say nothing), my Great Ones appear less glum. Finally they voice their agreement. Later Hapusoneb expresses his private opinion to me.

"With the Prince away, opposition to His Majesty will flag. This is an inspired move on His Majesty's part."

Well! Hapusoneb not being overly given to compliments, I am flattered.

The priesthood, however, is another matter. The support of Hapusoneb as First Prophet of Amon, and of Puyemre, Second Priest, I can count on. Since I appointed them both, their careers depend on my success. But the lesser high priests, who hold their offices through heredity or through wealthy and powerful influence, form a wall of antagonism. These are headed by my old friend Lord Rensonb, Third Priest of Amon, who, like all the priesthood, distrusts women in general and women rulers in particular. Needless to say, he is a firm exponent of the Prince.

Still, I rather welcome a confrontation with the Third Priest. To match wits with opposition is a challenge. As a woman—even a woman king—I cannot wrestle or race or fight with clubs. But my mind equals that of any man, and I relish a verbal battle if not a physical one.

Our audience is formidable. Rensonb is accompanied by three head priests, all as humorless and disapproving as he. As for him, he has worked himself up into a state of fanaticism.

"It has come to our ears, although we can scarcely credit the report, that His Majesty thinks to assign the Prince to a mining expedition."

"To accompany a group of priests of Amon to the Sinai to minister to the miners, yes."

"His Majesty"—Rensonb always slurs over the "His" as though the word pains him—"will actually send the heir to the throne into such *danger*? Perhaps to his *death*?" His eyes blaze like those of a furious tiger.

"All of life consists of danger," I return coldly.

"I speak of barbaric desert tribesmen, of venomous reptiles and insects, of insufferable heat, of a lack of amenities. The Prince is a mere boy, unused to hardship."

"But willing to endure it for Amon. My Majesty has spoken with the Prince. He is eager to embark on the venture."

"Little realizing what it entails." The eyes no longer flash, but gleam hard and cold as jasper. Surely the demons of the Underworld can be no uglier than the Third Priest.

He goes on. "Should aught befall the boy, the consequences will be overwhelming. Amon's servants will feel called on to protest this act of inhumanity."

Not only his words but his tone are ominous. He dares to threaten me, to hint of revolt. Oh, you little rabbit, you have gone too far! My temper overflows as boiling syrup does a cauldron.

"Pharaoh requires no advice from Third Priest or anyone else in this matter. Adequate precautions will be taken to protect the Prince. He wishes to go on the expedition. He will go. The Third Priest should learn to curb his tongue in the future. You are dismissed!" Now *my* eyes have turned to jasper.

The four priests prostrate themselves—what a temptation to stamp on each head as it lies before me—and back from the room. Rensonb has allowed his dyspepsia to overcome his reason. But this hostility signals the certainty of future battles.

119

Take warning, Hatshepsut. The Third Priest will undermine thy prestige in every way possible.

The thought so disturbs me that I feel an urge to discuss it, to divulge my perturbation to someone. Hapusoneb? He would view the matter coolly, dispassionately. Too dispassionately for my present mood. No, not Hapusoneb.

In my heart I know of only one in whom I wish to confide, to admit a womanly concern . . . one for whose voice, for whose thoughts, for whose encouragement I long. Hatshepsut, is this not a sign of weakness? Indeed yes, my heart. And so be it. I am a king . . . and I am also a woman.

I send for Senmut. He enters full of vigor and poise and confidence. His very presence calms my turmoil, as he first kneels, then stands before me.

For once I am awkward in introducing a subject.

"My Majesty desires your views on a matter," I begin. How pompous I sound.

"Yes, Majesty." He is courteous, attentive.

"Concerning the Prince and Lord Rensonb. You know Rensonb?"

"I know him, Majesty." His tone is noncommittal.

I am getting nowhere. Whatever was my purpose in summoning this man in the first place? I will make a fool of myself.

Be truthful, Hatshepsut. Thou wishedest his approval, his applause at thy account of besting Rensonb, at thy subduing of a worm of a man.

My cheeks burn. How low I have fallen. I will dismiss Senmut and . . .

Suddenly he is on his knees before me. "Gracious Majesty, know that I am your servant, true and faithful and ready till death. Any command, any wish, I will honor to my utmost strength. King you are. Equally important, you are a queen, my queen, second to none."

Rising, he lifts his eyes to mine. In them I see courage (for men can be beheaded for such daring words). And I see sincerity, sympathy, devotion . . . love. Yes, love.

All at once, and how it was managed I can never recall, we are in a close embrace.

"You are a bold man," I whisper.

"A man must be bold to adore a goddess," he whispers back.

My heart sings as wildly as a bird, as a star. He loves me, he loves me, he loves me!

Ah, Henut, you were right after all. I am the most fortunate of beings. And the happiest.

I am king of all Egypt—and the ruler of one man's heart. Prince, priests, Rensonb—defy me as you will. I have my comforter, my defender, my champion. Together, Senmut and I will conquer the world, the universe!

CHAPTER 11

Year 7 of the Reign
of His Majesty Makare Hatshepsut

Now in the year 7 of my reign, Thutmose is due to return at any time. During his absence his mother, Isis, has crept about her apartments like a frightened cat. My "Eyes and Ears," the Director of Royal Security, keeps close watch on her. Even feeble cats can scratch.

What we will do about the Prince now is a problem. I am doubtful about his remaining with the priesthood. There are too many restless elements there, young men yearning for intrigue who await only a cause, a leader. Above all, there is Lord Rensonb, who, like a buried seed, needs only a drop of water to burst from the soil. As yet I have found no way to oust him from No-Amon. His family and friends I cannot risk offending.

During Thutmose's absence the boy's name has come

up frequently at council meetings. Chief Royal Sealer Lord Snab, as stuffed with proposals as a goose with force-feeding, is forever inquiring, "Is the Princess Nefrure not soon to marry the Prince?"

And doubly ensure him a right to the throne, perhaps much sooner than I desire? Never. But *never* is a word to use sparingly with the council. I even encourage the belief that the two may eventually marry, since this hope will cool any inquiet throbs in rebellious hearts.

Meanwhile, my daughter develops well. Now eight years old, she is as exquisite as a lotus. At present her passion is her zoo. At one side of the palace is a fenced area with cages where Nefrure has been instructed to keep her pets. She is lax about this.

"I play with them in their quarters. Now it is their turn to visit *my* house," she says.

So cats, puppies, monkeys, ducks, geese, wander about the palace. Yesterday, as my Vizier was droning on about some domestic matter, there romped through the room a monkey holding a long feather aloft, a furiously squawking goose in hot pursuit. Hapusoneb ceased his recital and stood in disapproving silence until the two had disappeared down a passage.

This morning begins well, golden and turquoise, with a little whispering breeze. I recall the poem

Celebrate the glad day,
Be not weary therein.

For today is certain to be a glad day.

As soon as the morning's rituals are completed, I mount into my chariot. Yes. My *chariot*.

It is my dear Senmut who persuades me to try one— for pleasure. Chariots have been in use in Egypt for limited military maneuvers since my grandfather's time, and recently some of the young sons of the nobility have taken up chariot racing for sport. I believe the Prince enjoys this. Not that that is any recommendation.

"Just once thou shouldst attempt it!" Senmut suggests with enthusiasm. "One feels like a deer, so swiftly one moves. It is breathtaking. The pace creates a breeze, truly refreshing in the heat."

The novelty of the idea is appealing, even though I have not the fondness for horses that Senmut has. They seem to me willful and capricious. But a trusted servant, who shares Senmut's understanding of the animals, will drive, and I have only to hold on to the railing.

While this is primarily a ride for pleasure, it will also take us to my temple for a tour of inspection. I am dressed in my king's tunic, wearing the close-fitting blue crown that will, I hope, not go sailing off in the wind. Senmut rides in his chariot beside mine.

As usual he is proved to be right. Oh, the delight! There is nothing, I find, more exhilarating than flying down the road behind a spirited horse, the tranquil Nile on one side, the lofty red cliffs on the other.

I grip the leather strap and cry, "Faster! Faster! They will pass us!" as Senmut's chariot draws closer.

No one dares beat Pharaoh, but were anyone to attempt it, he would find he could not, could not, could not! I ride beside an experienced driver.

But . . . the driver drives. Senmut drives. Even Thutmose drives. Why should not Pharaoh drive?

I pull the reins from the man's hands. I, Hatshepsut, am in control of the fleetest horse in the land. What glory!

Far ahead of us dash the runners to clear the road of donkeys, stray goats, men carrying their yokes of pails or baskets, women with woven trays of produce balanced on their heads, children big and little.

"Earth, beware! The Great God Pharaoh approaches! On your knees!"

As I pass, the road is lined with heads lying in the dust like melons. A pharaoh observes more tops of heads than faces; would that more care were taken with the grooming of the hair. We Egyptians are proud of our large and liquid eyes, and yet Pharaoh is deprived of the sight of them.

At the river I rein in my horse, and Senmut's chariot draws up alongside mine. We gaze at each other and laugh.

"I was certain Her Majesty would enjoy the ride!" Senmut exclaims in triumph. (Him alone I permit to use "Her Majesty" in public. In private we are less formal.)

"Lord Senmut, one day I will find you wrong in

your opinion. What a downfall *that* will be," I tease him.

But no, he is never wrong in his ideas concerning me; his sympathy and understanding are endless. This man plays on my heart and mind as one does a harp, striking a rich chord at every touch.

Again, for no reason (or for every reason) we burst together into laughter. "Come," I say at length, "my temple awaits us."

Senmut helps me from the chariot. My boat waits at the bank to ferry us to the temple. The rows of sphinxes bordering the avenue should be completed by now, all of smooth rose granite, all wearing the head of Makare Hatshepsut. The palms and vines planted in the first courtyard will be flourishing.

"Could a day anywhere be more glorious than this?" I turn to Senmut, and he smiles his agreement.

Amon rides his golden chariot as I ride mine, across the dome of heaven. Oh, Amon, for this day I will raise thee soon two obelisks in thy temple!

On the opposite shore Senmut and I are borne in our chairs across the green fields as far as the first gate. As we descend, soldiers, officials, priests, radiate from us in a discreet protective circle.

"The setting is magnificent, Your Majesty." Senmut is trying to compose himself for the serious tour of my monument.

I hold in my own happiness. One's subjects expect solemnity rather than merriment from their sovereign.

Already people come in droves to watch the progress of the construction. For them vendors have set up stalls, selling religious offerings, flowers, scarabs, pottery cows, and bronze plaques of cows in honor of Hathor.

We stroll here and there. Most of the colonnades are in place on the first terrace. A pity that Egypt cannot produce myrrh trees for the terrace; then it could truly be a garden for Amon.

Senmut gestures toward the second terrace. "Majesty, look there. Along that portico is where twenty-six statues of Your Highness will stand. Those in the likeness of the Great God Osiris."

Yes, through the dust raised by the hammering and sawing of stone by the toiling workmen (for I have ordered they not discontinue their work in my presence), I can picture those statues. Just as I can picture the majesty of the completed monument. My heart is full. What pharaoh since the Great Pharaoh Chephren has discovered this inspired an architect to design his temple?

"Thy work pleases me greatly." I speak without thinking, but no one is near enough to hear my use of the intimate term.

Senmut bows low. "Her Majesty's words gladden my heart."

"In gratitude I have bestowed on thee collars and goblets of gold, and titles enough to weigh another man down. Hast thou now a wish, a desire that I may grant?"

With barely a moment's hesitation he answers eagerly. "I have a wish, yes. It is a fierce wish. One that thou mayest consider presumptuous."

"If so I will say so. Speak."

"Not only would it be an unparalleled honor to myself"—there is actually a nervous tremor in his voice—"it would ensure that I would dwell forever in the Hereafter as One's devoted and trusted servant."

How unlike Senmut, to shilly-shally around like a minor courtier.

He is trying my patience. Also my curiosity. "Speak, Senmut. Without fear."

"I thank thee. Know then that under Her Majesty's temple there is room to excavate a tomb. Her Majesty's own House of Eternity is located elsewhere. But if *I* could lie there . . . as the means to serve Her Majesty for eternity . . . I should be joyful beyond words."

Impassive or not, I am taken aback. It *is* a fierce wish. It *is* presumptuous. For I, not he, should have made the suggestion—if it were to be made at all. No one of the royal family would dare voice such a request.

As well as being a genius, Senmut is an audacious man. Have I not always said so? And I did offer him the opportunity. Still . . . the wish came quickly to his tongue. For how long has he nursed his desire?

He speaks true. I need this man now and I will need him forever, certainly in the fields of Ialu, in the shadowed land of Osiris, where I will not wish to wander alone. The closer he lies to me, the sooner his spirit will join mine. Only . . . I wish he had not been quite so ready with his appeal.

"In recognition of your outstanding services, Lord Senmut, I grant you your desire. Today I will have readied the scroll of authorization."

I speak graciously but with an air of reserve. Such requests are not to be made, let alone conceded, more than once in a lifetime. Even from a genius. Even from the love of my heart. Let my Unique Friend understand.

He is properly grateful. Senmut's confidence and self-respect I admire and occasionally resent as being too enormous for one mortal. At times they rival my own . . . and that I will not brook.

We return to No-Amon at midday. The morning has on the whole been a glad time. Ah, that swift ride behind a horse was rapture!

As soon as I enter the Great House, the Vizier's presence is announced. I am scraggly, coated with dust. My face feels as though the wind has blown off all its makeup, possibly some of its features as well. I have not even glanced into a mirror.

There is a sense of urgency in Hapusoneb's coming. Also in his appearance; his wig and usual placidity are both awry.

The bowing, kneeling, and ceremonial greetings dispensed with, Vizier comes to the point. "His Majesty could not have arrived at a more fortuitous moment. I hope to be the first to bear His Majesty the glad tidings."

"Glad tidings! My obelisks are come?"

The Vizier is disconcerted. "Not that I know of, Majesty. The tidings are of Prince Thutmose, who has this instant returned from his long and arduous assignment."

Am I supposed to twirl with joy, turn handsprings like an acrobat? I stare at Vizier. He stares at the floor, awaiting his cue.

I receive mine from him. Aware of my distrust of Thutmose, Hapusoneb still acts as though the tidings are indeed glad.

"My Majesty thanks you, Vizier," I say calmly. "A long and arduous journey, too, I expect. The Prince is well?"

My Vizier's tone is relieved. "In excellent health, Majesty." He bows, begins his retreat. "He will pay his respects to His Majesty soon. With His Majesty's permission . . ." He is gone.

CHAPTER 12

That very afternoon Thutmose waits on me. And brings with him no other than Lord Rensonb. A bad omen for our first interview. I assume the two kept in touch with each other for the three years of my stepson's retreat to the desert. Now Rensonb reappears as his foremost friend.

For the moment my eyes are on the Prince, who has just completed his fifteenth year. Far from returning weak or exhausted or diseased, he appears bursting with health, taller, tanner, more robust. And his nose—that, too, has grown. A true Thutmosid beak, wide and hooked, it dominates his face.

I wear my habitual serene expression. Pharaohs must mirror the aloofness of gods. Would that my inner spirit were always as tranquil.

"Gracious Pharaoh." He greets me with a low bow,

face and voice as emotionless as mine. I give him credit, he is a quick learner.

"Rise, Prince Thutmose. Thou art welcome again to No-Amon. Thou appearest well. The expedition was successful, the copper mines again at full production?"

"At full production." He was never one for words.

"Thy priestly duties were not onerous?"

"They were light. Our people being hardy and strong, all members of the group survived."

Does he believe I wished him not to survive? His eyes never leave the floor. Perhaps wisely. They might, like the uraeus on my crown, shoot me dead with their fire.

"One is delighted to hear it. So how didst thou employ thy time?"

"I practiced archery, I wrestled, I took part in chariot racing, I hunted."

"Very commendable."

Lord Rensonb clears his throat, and I sigh inwardly. Unfortunately, he *is* one for words.

"Your Majesty, I have made a suggestion to the Prince."

"Indeed?"

"As His Majesty is aware, an ancient and venerable tradition of our country is for a ruler to circuit the city of No-Amon in a chariot each New Year's Day. Like Amon's daily ride in his sun-chariot, it represents our ruler's continuing power and vitality."

I foresee what is coming. Oh, you are a sly rascal, Rensonb.

"A female monarch is by nature unfit for this type of exhibition. But the tradition is one that, for the prestige of Egypt before all her vassals, calls for continuance. Its lack has been noted in the past ten years. New Year's Day occurs in a few weeks. I propose that Prince Thutmose is eminently qualified to make the tour at that time."

Rensonb's expression is that of a lion that has just devoured a plump kid.

"The Prince not being a ruler," I remark dryly, "it is an inappropriate and foolish suggestion. Dost thou not agree, my son?"

"At this particular time it may have little meaning," Thutmose answers sedately.

Was the proposition his or Rensonb's? His expression tells me nothing.

Rensonb flushes scarlet as a poppy. Likely his poor stomach has turned that color, too.

"The symbolism is what is significant," he hisses. How he does delight in hissing—like a snake. "The envoys, the people, miss this colorful and representative event."

"In that case My Majesty will be happy to circle the bounds of No-Amon this New Year," I say carelessly.

"In a *chariot*?" Rensonb is incredulous.

"Certainly in a chariot. Do you not know My Majesty drives his own chariot?"

My gratification at his crestfallen expression is interrupted. There is a commotion in the antechamber. Without waiting to be announced, Senmut bursts into the room.

"The obelisks . . ." He is panting with exertion as if he has run a good distance. "The obelisks . . . Her Majesty ordered from . . . the quarries of Elephantine . . . they arrive. O Majesty. . . . Already they have passed . . . the great temple. . . . If you . . . His . . . Her Majesty will step to the balcony . . . The rafts are within sight." He is so excited he is incoherent. But his meaning is clear.

With unserene step I make for the balcony, Senmut, the Prince, and Rensonb behind. Such a sight! Toward me approach three rows of vessels, nine vessels to a row, the oarsmen rowing furiously. I can hear the piping of flutes, the beating of drums that set the rhythm.

"Nine hundred sixty oarsmen, Majesty!" Senmut breathes.

Towed by the boats is a tremendous barge—three hundred feet long, Senmut informs me—bearing the two gigantic obelisks of pink granite, resting base to base.

"Each monument of *one* block of stone. Each to soar one hundred feet into the air!" Senmut is beside himself. "And both excavated and transported in a mere season's time."

The other windows of the palace are crammed with heads and waving arms. Up and down the riverbanks onlookers cluster, staring in awe. Thutmose and Rensonb stand in silence behind me.

"And now," I remark proudly, "they are ready to be polished, inscribed, and raised, with no more than seven months to elapse from the beginning of work to the end. There can be no better builders anywhere, ever, than our own!"

And no better a country to glorify than my Egypt. The tops of the monuments will be gilded with gold. They will dazzle the eye, gleam as brightly as Amon's chariot in the heavens. Already in my mind are the words of the inscription:

And you who after long years shall see these monuments, who shall speak of what I have done, you will say 'we do not know how they can have made a whole monument of gold as if it were an ordinary task.' To gild them I have given gold measured by the bushel, as though it were sacks of grain. And when my majesty had said the amount it was more than the whole of the Two Lands had ever seen. . . . When you shall hear this, do not say that this is an idle boast, but 'How like her this was, worthy of her father! . . .'

Senmut's voice breaks into my thoughts. "Where are they to stand, Majesty?"

"I have not decided. Perhaps in the third courtyard of Amon's temple."

They shall stand where they will most honor my father and myself. Unfortunately, the highest point of the temple is the tremendous indoor hall; the next highest is the third courtyard. Well, I have a week or two to make that decision.

The flotilla has passed; the river ripples in the wake of the great raft. Like the ripples, people fan out from their clusters to go about their business.

Thutmose and Lord Rensonb bow themselves away, Rensonb somewhat subdued, my stepson as self-contained as ever. At one point I believe I heard Rensonb mutter, "More obelisks," as though they grew on trees like pomegranates. But then he is feeling frustrated. A thought jars me: Of the two, the youth is far more astute than the man. I wonder what *his* plans are for the future.

Turning to a more pleasant subject, I reflect with satisfaction on my promise to restore and build more fine monuments for the Two Lands. Shortly the pair of obelisks will point toward the sun. They constitute a triumph for me; they will be a major achievement of my reign. Through the ages they will prove what a woman king is capable of!

Perhaps that triumph made me overconfident—or at least unwary and relaxed, a state I will never again fall into. For a few days later occurred, to offset that victory, a defeat and humiliation such as I have never experienced. So horrendous it was that I still claw my hair in the agony of remembrance.

On a minor feast day I, with my court, am present in the main hall of Amon's temple. For the occasion

I am wearing the king's kilt, with beard fastened to my chin, the tail of a giraffe tied about my waist, and on my head the white crown of Upper Egypt.

I stand slightly in front of the nobles to watch the arrival of Amon's image borne on its litter. After circling the hall, the priests escorting the litter will conduct me to the Station of the King, the post reserved for Pharaoh.

As I wait more or less patiently (these ceremonies take place so regularly that my mind tends to wander), I notice Thutmose on his knees before a small altar, burning incense to Amon. Ah, I reflect with approval, Hapusoneb has succeeded after all; he has shaped an acceptable priest of the Prince.

The body of priests enters, approaches. They bear on their shoulders the magnificent boat, gilded, with inlays of ebony and ivory. Red-and-gold hangings are drawn round the sides to shield the image from public view. Only I and certain high priests are permitted to view the god, who usually dwells in the holy-of-holies.

The procession continues innocently enough, the shaven-headed priests in their white robes chanting hymns and swinging salvers of incense. I am not fully attentive, my mind adrift.

A few gasps from the nobles draw my attention. The procession is circling the hall, not at its usual stately pace, but weaving erratically between and around the columns as though in search of something or someone. My first impression is that the priests are tipsy.

On a holiday they have consumed too much wine. Or else the heat has affected them. I gasp myself. If Amon's ark should be dropped, what disaster!

I can feel the entire court holding its breath. At least no one dreams or dozes. All eyes are on Amon's boat.

Thutmose, I notice, has drawn back from the niche and is gazing with astonishment at the rambling line of priests. I have to admit, I believe he is quite ignorant of what is about to happen. Either that or he acts extremely well, which is conceivable.

Nearing the Prince, the file comes to a sudden halt. All bend forward in an eerie sort of manner, as if a high wind has pushed them . . . or as if Amon's hand has been heavy on their backs. They, with Amon's bark, appear to *bow* to Thutmose.

The Prince prostrates himself, a look of stunned reverence on his face. Head to floor, he waits. Ah, ah, ah . . . I incline to judge he *is* a consummate actor.

One of the priests raises him. He is somehow maneuvered into the center of the group, which then pursues its course . . . but not toward me, as is expected, but onward to the Station of the King. In my place, where only Pharaoh may stand, is deposited . . . the Prince! Quite smoothly the priests with Amon's image glide to their own accustomed stations.

The unthinkable has happened. For an instant my head whirls, my blood ceases to flow. For only an instant.

I give the boy no chance to lead the ritualistic responses. In a clear voice *I* make them. *I* offer the

138

customary oblation. *I* signal the end of the service.

I might be alone in the temple, the silence is so deep. None of the courtiers moves, no one utters a murmur. As I sweep from the hall I send the Prince a terrible look. He pretends not to see, his gaze fixed on the dark passageway where Amon's boat has retreated.

This . . . this impudence I will deal with, but not here, not now. There is a banquet at the palace at midday, another service at the temple, a ceremony at the Window of Appearances. Pharaoh is expected to be present at all of these. And he shall be! *No* one will realize the effect of his affront, no one. After all that I have enacted for the priesthood . . . oh, it is an outrage.

I manage. At the feast I chatter coolly with Hapusoneb and Nehesi, both of whom are so nervous they stutter and repeat themselves like parrots. Their babbling is almost amusing. I believe they are concerned lest I break into tears. Tears! I, Makare Hatshepsut, have not wept since I was a child.

My animation covers my complete lack of appetite. The temple service goes off smoothly. At the Window of Appearances I toss the goblets and necklaces with an automatic smile.

This is made easier by Nefrure's presence. She is wholly at ease with the public, waving and blowing them kisses. Today, as though trying to cheer me, she sparkles more than usual.

"Mother, wilt thou allow me to throw the chain to

Lord Nok?" (Nok is a yellowish old man of the aristocracy who permits Nefrure, and no one else, to order him about.)

"Yes, do so. That will please him."

While I watch the proceedings, my mind is busy. Surely Rensonb is the instigator of this impertinence, this insult. Would that he could be flogged, banished to the mines, burned to ashes. But the priests will insist that the performance was Amon's will, that they simply bow to his command. Ah, they are clever. Still, I am not one to be bested—by anyone.

Nefrure glances at me inquiringly. "What is it?" I whisper.

"I threw Nok's necklace. He barely caught it. May I throw another?"

"No, my daughter, that is enough. Stand beside me while I present the others."

And finally my public duties are over. I send for Senmut, who has been to Abydos on pilgrimage. He comes at once.

On landing at No-Amon he was told the story. How my people do love to gossip. Discretion is not part of their nature.

I describe the event. "This is more than Rensonb alone. All the priests in that procession—I should like to have them deported. But the priesthood would never name them. I cannot risk humiliation by asking."

For once Senmut is shocked into silence.

"Is it a rebellion? Who—besides Rensonb—is behind it?" I muse aloud. "My 'Eyes and Ears' had no warning of the act."

"Majesty . . ."

"Speak."

"Surely this was engineered by the Prince himself? He gains most by the mockery."

Senmut has never trusted Thutmose. And I suspect my stepson has little liking for my Sole Companion. But I would swear the act caught the Prince by surprise.

"I think not. Another thing is certain. It is not an act of good faith by the priests. Amon would never turn against me. It is a cunning trick to undermine my authority."

"Then the priesthood is to blame," Senmut admits reluctantly.

"Their greed for land, cattle, slaves, revenue, gold, is unending. The head priests of Amon hint constantly that higher taxes must be levied on fields, crops, mines. Recently I demurred: 'Let the people have a holiday from taxation,' I told them. Perhaps this is their answer: They threaten to usurp me."

Senmut looks worried. "True, the priesthood continues to grow in power."

Yes. Their power increases. Even Father feared and distrusted them. Well, I must puncture their authority before it overwhelms my own.

Loyal to me as he is, ready to war against anyone else, Senmut will never willingly oppose the clergy. At heart he is still a peasant. And peasants believe that only the talismans, the amulets, the magic of the priests can make life and the afterlife secure for them. The priesthood, capitalizing on this simplicity of most of my people, encourages fear and superstition.

I find I am quivering with rage. The presumption! How dare they? In Pharaoh's very presence to set that boy in *my* seat—to abase me before all my court! I have been generous to Amon's priesthood, and this is my repayment.

Yet even *I* cannot take on the entire priesthood. Or can I? My mind races, grasps the seed of an idea. . . . Yes, it will do!

"I have new orders for you, Senmut." My heart still pounds within me like a drum, but my voice is calm, icy.

He is startled. "Yes, Majesty?"

"I have determined on the location of my obelisks. They will stand in the great hall of Amon's temple. The very hall where that shameful exhibition took place today."

My cool and collected Senmut is aghast. "B-but . . . are they not much too tall for the hall?"

"Exactly. So the roof will be demolished. I am sure my holy father Amon would prefer them to stand in the highest court of his temple . . . and out of doors, too. What the priests prefer I care not."

All at once I am in great good humor. I have paid back the clergy for their stupid trick. My obelisks will be placed on the finest, the highest site of the temple.

And the threat of Thutmose's opposition, which I have vaguely sensed since his return from the Sinai, will collapse like a bubble. All is well for now.

Yes, for now. Be content, Hatshepsut. Do not seek further trouble for today. There will be ample tomorrow.

CHAPTER 13

Year 9 of the Reign
of His Majesty Makare Hatshepsut

This year so far is one of peace and prosperity. As on a voyage down the Nile, without wind to obstruct, I cleave the water swiftly and smoothly. Egypt's storerooms are packed with grain. Our neighbors are on friendly (more or less) terms.

Still, I do not suffer from perfect placidity. My "Eyes and Ears" overflows with vague but disturbing rumors.

"The Prince," he declares to me in my small audience chamber, "is said to grow restless and moody with discontent. He finds his priestly duties tedious and wishes for action—of one sort or another."

I sigh. "Surely there are pastimes aplenty in Egypt. He could hunt lions, which sport combines action *and* risk. Or amuse himself with girls, an even more perilous pursuit."

My "Eyes and Ears" smiles obediently, then becomes serious. "The lord Rensonb confers with the Prince at night. They speak intently for long hours. On what topics we cannot ascertain."

"Strategy of the *senet* board, perhaps. Or which men to bet on at the wrestling matches."

Despite my frivolous remarks, I take heed of my spy's words. I err always on the side of caution.

"To be of worth, the news must be more definite."

"We will do our utmost, gracious Highness."

In my mind there is one great idea that grows as rapidly as Egypt's corn. If the project comes to fruition, it will strengthen my position before all of the Two Lands, and in particular before my stepson.

For some time I have toyed with the idea of mounting a sailing expedition to Punt, that mysterious land lying at the southernmost tip of the world. There are several reasons in favor of this, apart from that of exalting my prestige.

One: Were I a male king, I should judge this the proper moment for a military campaign of some sort. Now and then Pharaoh's strength must be paraded before both foreign countries and our own people.

Two: Long ago I promised my divine father Amon-Re to create for him a garden of Punt in my temple. To fulfill this obligation, Senmut proposes incense trees for the main terrace. It is an inspired suggestion. The best of these trees are to be found in Punt.

Senmut agrees the expedition would have value; he adds a third reason. With better-than-average inundations the past few years, my Black Land's internal affairs are in excellent order. So excellent that the people grow bored—a condition unfolding more often from contentment than from discontent. How contrary humans are. In any case, a new and challenging project is needed to stir their interest.

True, in the distant past, journeys to Punt were made by water. But they were small, haphazard affairs. Mine will be large and well organized, with scientists to observe the weather, the stars, the foibles of the sea, the fauna and flora of Punt. And there will be scribes and artists along to record all observations.

How I long to head such an expedition myself! Admit it, Hatshepsut (as thou always hast), being a woman is not entirely fortunate. If I were a man I should be away tomorrow, leading troops to Syria or Libya or Cush, warships to Crete, Cyprus, Byblos. The Great Green would hold no terrors for me. To view new lands, new faces, new customs—what rapture! For I thrive on novelty and adventure.

Nonetheless, facing the truth, I am forced also to face that figure who, like a bad spirit, skulks in my shadow: Thutmose III. He is forever *there*, and I am aware of his presence as I am of an irremovable carbuncle. And being there, he must be watched constantly.

Nearing eighteen, the Prince is at a dangerous age: impatient, impetuous, invincible, and in his case possessing a magnetic quality that, despite his reserve, draws others to him. The Prince feels, I am told, that

I deprived him of his rights when I ascended the throne. What nonsense! What rights has he? My husband, whose own blood was only half divine, named the boy his successor and thereby swelled his head to the size of a watermelon. Rights indeed!

While making his devotions in Amon's temple, my stepson is attended by a head priest loyal to me. In the Great House he is the target of many eyes, in particular those of the Vizier.

But others watch as well. Others who have not my, but his, interests at heart. Ruefully I have to concede: A year's absence from the Two Lands would be a grave mistake. Against my will I shall remain at home for the protection of my throne.

"Who shall lead the the expedition to God's Land?" I ask Senmut.

We discuss various officials.

Senmut smiles at me. "It must be a man interested in finance, since it is a trading venture. A man who is devoted to Her Majesty and who receives complete devotion from his own subordinates. A man efficient at organization. Canst thou guess the riddle?"

I smile back. "No need to guess. There is only one who fills all counts. Nehesi the Nubian. Yes, he is the perfect choice."

What would I ever do without Senmut? I said once that even a male pharaoh needs someone to understand him, to share his most intimate thoughts, to love him. I have that someone, to whom I can speak of anything, of whom I can ask advice, whom I can order (no, not order, request) to perform any task and have it flawlessly performed. I depend on him as a daughter does a father; a wife, a husband. Far more than I ever depended on Thutmose II.

Senmut now has his own apartments in the palace. When he moved into them two years ago, my court was scandalized.

"A nobody born of nobodies."

"What a flouting of tradition, an upstart to be honored above my husband who, as is known everywhere, is the most hardworking, most self-sacrificing, most loyal . . ."

"The uncrowned Pharaoh of the Two Lands."

These and worse were whispered and sneered through the court. It soon ended. Unorthodox acts are almost expected of a queen who has made herself king. Nothing could be more scandalizing than *that*.

"As the expedition is planned for Amon's glory, I must ask Amon's approval," I remark.

Senmut is in full accord. In his chapel is a shrine to Amon and to Amon's wife, Mut (Senmut's patron goddess), to whom he prays frequently. "The gods have blessed the Two Lands. They have blessed me above all men. I am grateful."

The following morning I exact my privilege to "feed the god" in place of one of the high priests. Dressed in the simple robe of a priest, a leopard hide fastened over my shoulder, I enter the holy-of-holies in the heart of the Great Temple. It is a ceremony I usually avoid. As we pass softly from the main court through the dimness of the long hall to the dimmer antechamber to the utter darkness of Amon's sanctuary, the air clogged with incense, candles flickering like the tongues of serpents, the low chanting of hymns by the priests around me, I wonder eerily, Am I alive in my own body? Or have I changed to my *ka*, and as a spirit do I approach the Underworld?

What fancies, Hatshepsut! Thou art Pharaoh—the most resolute and unfanciful of pharaohs!

At the door of the shrine I break the clay seal and enter. From its niche I draw forth the jeweled gold figure of the god, remove its robe of fine linen stiffened with golden threads, wash the figure, and reclothe it. I set it on a high stand, and from two priests standing just outside the shrine I take silver dishes of delicacies and place these before Amon. While the god absorbs his sustenance by magic, I await some token of his desire.

"Great God of Gods," I pray, "is it to thy liking that I send an expedition to Punt? Grant me a sign, O my divine Father."

A blob of wax drops from a candle, making it flare wildly. Amon's arm appears to rise, then fall.

Into my heart comes his message of approval. "Go, my daughter. Search out the highways to the myrrh terraces. They are a glorious region of God's Land, that place which I created to divert my heart."

The words are clear. I stand as in a trance, scarcely breathing, wreathed in a heavy cloak of incense, my eyes on the golden image. Finally the spell lifts and I back from the shrine. The High Priest sweeps away my footprints with a palm leaf, then closes the door and reseals it.

The priests and my council accept Amon's sanction of the expedition. We can proceed.

Eight ships are ordered. They are shaped somewhat like Oriental slippers, the long toe curving up and inward. The toe is the stern, with a rudder on either side. The bow has for its figurehead a high carved ram, in honor of Amon. The sail, twice as wide as it is high, is woven in a bright geometric pattern. Since the hulls, the rudders, and the broad oars curved like swords are all painted in colored designs, the ships resemble a swarm of butterflies alight on the water.

The head shipbuilder has fashioned a model for Nefrure; it is an exact replica of one of the vessels. My daughter goes scarlet with bliss.

"Oh, I thank you, Zau. Many times I thank you. It is beautiful and I will treasure it forever, to remind me of you and of Egypt's fleet!"

Zau is as rosy and pleased as Nefrure. He has reason to be. The vessels appear staunch and smart and proud as swans.

They are loaded with goods to barter: lengths of linen (for flax is not so easily grown outside the Two Lands); mirrors (barbarians surely delight in admiring their own faces as much as civilized folk); beads of faience and bracelets of copper; sandals and mats and ropes of papyrus; rolls of papyrus paper for writing;

a few pieces of fine stoneware and a set of gold dinnerware for the King of Punt.

In spite of our people's fear of leaving Egypt, there is no lack of volunteers to man *this* expedition: scribes, government officials, soldiers for protection, above all, sailors. Nehesi has insisted these latter be experienced: "Men who had seen the sky, who had seen the earth, who were more prudent than wild animals, who could foretell the coming of the storm before it broke."

On the day of departure the docks are so crowded I wonder that the planks do not collapse under the weight of the spectators. Relatives scream and wave, weeping one moment, laughing the next. Vendors of meat and cakes push through the throng, hoarsely calling their wares. Children wail. Everyone sweats, pants with thirst, limps with sore feet, grumbles at the crush, loses his children, has his pocket picked and his lunch knocked from his hand, and would exchange his situation with no one.

Space on the main quay is roped off and a throne readied for me. I watch the priests make the propitiary offerings to Hathor and to the goddesses of the air, with a plea for wind for the journey. And finally I ask Amon's blessing on the fleet for its long voyage.

They are off, sailing down the Nile as far as the delta, then turning into the canal of Wady Tumilat, which leads to the sea.

"The gods be with you, ships! Fair journey and safe return," I whisper. This day I would gladly—almost—

change places with the lowliest sailor aboard one of the vessels.

Later, when I tell this to Senmut, he shakes his head. "The Great Green on occasion sets up a strange motion on ships. One can feel ill to the point of dying— or wishing for death. And this movement can last for the entire voyage."

"Others may feel ill. Pharaoh would not," I retort. Imagine, wishing for death on an exciting journey! Common people are by nature weaker than pharaohs.

With the Punt venture out of the way for the time being, I can devote thought to the Prince and what to do with him. That problem is brought unexpectedly to a head when Lord Rensonb requests an audience. Surely the subject will be Thutmose, whose champion Rensonb is.

After polite and insincere greetings are exchanged, the lord comes to the point.

"His Majesty is aware that Lord Put, Head Priest at Hikuptah, has lately died."

I incline my head.

"After a year's illness he has left the temple there in great disarray. A conscientious man is needed to set affairs in order."

"And you wish to propose . . ."

"The prince Thutmose. His work in the Great Temple is outstanding."

My impression is that Thutmose's prowess at sports is far more outstanding than his temple efforts, but I will let that pass. The idea seems innocuous enough . . . except that Lord Rensonb has suggested it. Any plan of his will not have *my* welfare at heart.

"My Majesty will consider your request. This meets with the Prince's approval?"

"Prince Thutmose is eager to go wherever Amon has need of him," Rensonb declares loftily. He bows himself out, shoulders high as if he had just won the first move of *senet*.

I ponder. While a transfer to Hikuptah would take my stepson away from his partisans at No-Amon, surely he would encounter others as strong at Egypt's second city. At Hikuptah there is no Hapusoneb, no Puyemre, to hold a rein on the boy. Treasonous plotting could take place unhindered. Still . . . still . . . the boy would be out of my sight and away from the seat of power. And yes! His mother, Isis, under my eye in the palace, would serve as hostage for her son's loyalty. Had Rensonb not appeared so self-satisfied . . . Well, I will make a decision after my river trip to Akhmim.

My excuse is to inspect the irrigation system at this town and cut the first sod of a new canal. Mainly I wish for once to be lazy, to sit in a boat under a canopy and watch Egypt's landscape slide past, to contemplate my kingdom. Senmut will accompany me.

On the day we leave, a wind scoops scallops from the river, whips trees into tangles, sends flocks of kites to soar and swoop and scream mournfully. Traveling with the current, we sail against the wind, so the oarsmen pull and strain, keeping time to the flute as perfectly as temple dancers. Still we make small progress. Little matter. Drowsily I regard the life of the river. Women wash their clothes at the bank, smacking the cloth against the rocks, chattering like crows. They stare curiously at my barge (shipmaster makes frantic signs at them to bow; his gestures amuse them into gales of laughter). Farmers work their *shadufs* to lift water from the river up to the canals lacing their fields. Small boys dangle fishlines.

Other boats, as varied in species as birds, crowd the river: papyrus skiffs, large fishing boats trailing seines, cumbersome ferries, merchantmen from Hikuptah or Crete or the Lebanon, rafts piled high with grain or produce, barges loaded with timber from Byblos or granite from Aswan, pleasure craft with high curved prows, like the graceful necks of herons. On the rudders of a towing boat two immense blue-and-white eyes, painted there for the craft's protection, glare at us.

As we glide past a swampy area of reeds and papyrus, I ask Senmut, "Didst thou ever go fowling as a child?"

"Often. I was lucky with the throw stick. Almost always I brought home a bag of ten ducks or more. And thou?"

I laugh at a sudden remembrance. "Once, on the way home from a fowling excursion, Father and my brothers and I stopped at one of the royal estates to see grapes being pressed for wine. There were six stone vats over which hung a number of ropes. Holding on to these, the pickers trod out the grapes. As they worked they sang lustily, as all laborers do, or at least they sang till they ran out of breath."

"Thou paintest a cheerful picture," Senmut remarks with a smile.

"I was fascinated. I begged my father, 'More than anything in the world I should like to join those men in the vats. Oh, please, Father, let me jump on the grapes!'

"Father hesitated—he usually enjoyed my strange whims (which my two brothers were too conventional to voice)—but then he answered, 'Hatshepsut, what would thy mother say? A princess with purple legs and feet!'

" 'But yes, Father!' I cried with glee. 'It will set a new fashion at court!'

"He laughed and diverted my attention to a sack of grape skins being twisted to extract more juice. So treading grapes is a pleasure I have never indulged in."

The ceremony of the canal opening at Akhmim goes well. We are housed in the Governor's mansion for two nights, entertained with the usual receptions and banquets.

The conversation is the ordinary light chatter until the Governor, a genial but rather simple man, remarks, "So His Majesty is about to lose the lady Isis. A pity her health deteriorates. I understand she is a sympathetic person—as His Majesty knows." He smiles broadly, quite innocent of his shocking statement.

Senmut asks quickly, "How did you learn of this, Lord? The affair has been kept quiet."

The Governor looks dismayed. "I . . . I mention it for His Majesty's ears alone. Some priest or other . . . no, it was a representative of Lord Rensonb, who recently stayed here the night. He was sent to make arrangements for the lady Isis in Hikuptah. Ah, now I remember, he cautioned me not to refer to it! I hope . . . I hope . . ."

"But certainly," Senmut soothes him. "Very right you are. I merely wondered." Catching my eye, he twists his mouth wryly.

Our trip home is made speedily, the wind captured in our huge square sail embroidered with lotus blossoms. We approach No-Amon, the pennants bright as poppies snapping in the wind, the gleaming spires, among them the glittering tops of my obelisks, the high walls and pylons and carved pillars of Amon's temple. It is a brave sight, but one which for once I scarcely notice.

CHAPTER 14

An hour after my arrival at the Great House I summon Lord Rensonb. This time we waste no time in idle greetings.

"Why is there such secrecy in the plan to remove the lady Isis to Hikuptah? Why was My Majesty not informed of her poor health?"

Rensonb's expression is as stolid as mine, but his blood, rising to his face, betrays him.

"There is no secrecy in the matter, Your Majesty," he returns stiffly.

"Then why did you not mention it at our last audience?"

"It was an oversight." His tone is sullen.

My temper is rising out of control. Take care, Hatshepsut. Thou canst not accuse this man of treason without proof, and he is too clever to furnish thee *that*.

"Hear My Majesty's reply to your recent request. Prince Thutmose is not sufficiently experienced to take charge of the temple at Hikuptah. His duties in the Great Temple are carelessly performed, I am told."

"The Prince is afforded no scope for his talents." Rensonb's voice is hoarse with rage. He can afford to be officious. Were I to chastise him, I would offend the greater part of No-Amon's priesthood.

"We will find him a position with scope. You may leave."

He does so, his body atremble. Oh, how I hope his wretched stomach suffers from this interview.

With Thutmose and his mother both in Hikuptah, surely there was some plot afoot. I put some inquiries into motion . . . and wait.

Life goes on as usual. Nefrure studies the lyre with dedication. When I visit her apartments I find her plucking the strings and singing softly. More and more she performs in temple ceremonies, shaking the sistrum and joining the other priestesses in choral chanting. Whether my daughter will become another pharaoh I doubt; she lacks the drive and desire. But she will make an affectionate and gracious queen on Egypt's throne.

For whom? the court wonders, although it stifles the question in my presence. I dangle Nefrure before them as a possible prize for Thutmose—as long as he continues to behave. It is a powerful incentive. In two or three years, when my daughter is twelve or thirteen, Thutmose could become pharaoh by marrying her, the right to the throne carried always by women.

Only Senmut knows my convictions. Despite court and council, despite the simple logic of such a match, Nefrure will never marry the Prince. Not so long as I live. I do not lean toward a man so clearly hostile to me.

Thutmose avoids me, holds no audience with me. Now and then I glimpse him in the palace gardens at a distance. He strolls with his mother, who, while no doubt as healthy as I, more and more resembles a frail cloud of smoke. There is no substance to her, never was; who would expect it in a mere concubine? I must admit, the Prince possesses an overabundance of substance. Why could he not have resembled his parents, with their weak constitutions, their pallid indecision?

My "Eyes and Ears," instructed to increase his vigilance, comes often to report. "The Prince sees less of Lord Rensonb. And more of young women—some ladies, some not, none of a serious nature. He fulfills his priestly duties more efficiently than formerly, if not enthusiastically."

"What *does* he do enthusiastically?"

"He bends the bow, heaves the spear, swims powerfully, runs like a gazelle, drives a chariot with verve."

"The complete athlete."

"Indeed, Majesty, he is extraordinarily proficient in sports. He even takes pleasure in riding astride a horse."

"A silly achievement. Well. Continue to monitor all aspects of his life. Report any friendships, any meetings, any contacts the Prince forms anywhere."

My "Eyes and Ears" struts with importance. His force of spies now nearly equals the army in size and is far more active. We will hope it is effective.

The Nile shrinks to a thread, then spreads wide with a new inundation, a good one, and another New Year's Day is here. I look forward to viewing the artwork created this past year in the royal workshops and displayed in the great hall: vases and statues and jewelry and tapestries and finely crafted weapons. After I and Senmut and my daughter choose what we wish for our tombs, the Prince selects what he desires—and then Isis. I cannot gainsay Thutmose, who considers his mother a member of the royal family, which of course she is not. The rest of the items are dispatched to foreign potentates as tokens of Egypt's friendship.

I grow more and more impatient regarding my expedition to Punt. A messenger was to have disembarked on the return trip on the shore of the Great Green, to make his way across the red land and bring me news. There is a desert road by way of the Wady Hammamat connecting No-Amon with various mines. Along the way are buried enormous jars of water.

To my joy, one afternoon the messenger arrives. He is covered with red grit and holds out a tightly rolled scroll. As I unroll it with shaking hands, a quick thought passes through my head: Tutami's lessons in reading were worth every miserable moment spent in his classroom.

The messenger waits, head to ground. I order food and drink brought him, command him to eat in my presence (he cannot, being too nervous, but does gulp a jugful of wine), where he can answer my questions.

Yes, the expedition has been thoroughly satisfactory and should reach No-Amon in another month or so.

"And the shrine?" I demand, too impatient to search out the answer in the scroll. "Was a shrine to Amon set up in God's Land?"

The messenger bends to the floor again, perhaps happier, after his long course, in that position than standing. "Indeed so. A shrine to the Great God Amon and to His Majesty the Great God Pharaoh was established in Punt before any other event."

Content, I settle back to read the letter.

The voyage had been a long one but with no violent storms, no confrontation by enemy ships. While the vessels were anchored at night, there were no attacks by desert raiders.

Sea monsters were glimpsed and described: huge fish with sharp teeth, and, caught in a net, a horrid creature with eight arms, each the size and length of a cobra. Every arm was capable of winding itself about a man and conveying him to the creature's dreadful mouth, which, large as a cavern, could envelop him whole. I shiver with horror.

There were other tremendous fish, but good-natured

and playful, which somersaulted through the water and grinned up at the watching sailors. The weather being warm and disagreeably damp, the men dripped always with perspiration. Some developed a rash over their bodies due to the unaccustomed moisture, but this, while itchy and uncomfortable, produced no lasting effects.

I read on:

Our arrival at Punt—ah, would that His Majesty had been present!—was an event never to be forgotten. We dropped anchor in a bay, the shore crowded with palm-roofed huts standing on piles. From the dwellings streamed the natives in great awe, men of broad shoulders and braided beards, with their wives and children.

Forth strode the King of the Puntites, Perehu, to welcome me as I waited at the head of my guard. Behind His Highness followed his queen (a woman more encased in fat than a hippopotamus, so prodigious she could hardly move), mounted on a donkey which threatened at any instant to collapse.

Their greeting was astonished and joyous and at once they asked, "Why have you come here to this land which few men know? Are you from the sky or the earth? How have you traveled, over land, over water, or through the air? The touch of your feet causes the earth to be fertile. And for His Gracious Majesty of Tomery (Egypt), we live by the breath he bestows on us."

Having pitched our tents, we offered Their Majesties refreshments from the Two Lands. After, our articles of barter were set out, which caused much exultation among the people. Their Majesties expressed deep gratification at His Majesty's gifts and at once had goods brought out for exchange.

These we loaded into our vessels, all fine fragrant woods of God's Land, bundles of myrrh-resin, fresh myrrh-trees, blackest ebony and purest ivory, cinnamon-wood, incense, eye-cosmetic, living creatures such as baboons, monkeys and dogs, skins of the southern panther, even natives and their children. Never was the like of this brought for any king since the beginning of Egypt. His Majesty will, I believe, be highly pleased.

And now we have set sail from God's Land. Soon we will disembark His Majesty's messenger, who bears this letter and all good wishes for His Majesty's health and happiness from her servant Nehesi.

I laugh with joy and triumph. From the hand of an attendant I take a heavy gold necklace and clasp it about the neck of the messenger.

"This, for your good news," I tell him. "Now let us hope for the fleet's safe and speedy return!"

It turns out to be a safe return, although not so speedy as I should have liked. But one afternoon I am informed that in two days' time the ships will dock at No-Amon. The whole court is in an uproar.

In the middle of it all, my "Eyes and Ears" enters

the chamber wearing his most woeful (and favorite) expression.

"Gracious Majesty, there is mischief about."

"What sort of mischief?"

"It appears . . . there is brewing some sort of plot. Known troublemakers have met with members of Amon's priesthood. Gold has been transferred. The troublemakers have been arrested, questioned—with the help of cudgels—and they know nothing. They insist they work for others whose names they confessed. Those others cannot be found. They have fled to the sand dwellers."

They are clever, my enemies. In particular Lord Rensonb. And of course the Prince. Their involvement will not easily be traced.

"You keep a watch on Lord Rensonb and all suspicious priests?"

"Indeed yes, gracious Majesty. Anyone even slightly suspected of harm is watched."

I, too, watch. I watch my servants, my courtiers, the priests, my guard. There are few—as few as the fingers of one hand—whom I trust completely. Beyond this my fate must lie in Amon's hands. But I am too excited by the coming event to worry overmuch.

The Chief Steward, believing I wish to receive Lord Nehesi and the Puntites in the Great House, has the staff prepare the main reception hall, polishing the floor, repainting friezes, renewing upholstery.

"Certainly not," I tell him. "The thanksgiving ceremony will take place at dockside. My Majesty has no intention of missing the excitement." How Steward's face falls.

So it is all to do over: a throne set up on a section of the quays, two chairs beside it, a stool slightly behind for Nefrure, a stretch of matting to extend between the dock and my throne, canopies and awnings installed, along with tables for refreshments. I take my seat, Senmut beside me.

What elation, to sight the first ship, watch the fleet glide like proud birds to the dock, amid crowds of people shrieking and waving in jubilation. The gangplank of the flagship is run out, and down it marches Nehesi, erect and smiling.

Choked with emotion he kneels before me. "Your Majesty . . . we have completed our quest . . . with success. . . . Behold . . . myrrh trees for His Majesty's temple . . . His Majesty's subjects from Punt . . ."

Around his neck I hang the Gold of Valor; for his noteworthy service I award him a grant of land, tax free. Then with him and Senmut in places of honor beside me, I greet our Puntite visitors, wave them to seats close by.

Finally, the sight which I have been awaiting for more than a year, the procession of bearers transporting the loads of wood and ivory and hides and animals. Myrrh is heaped in piles taller than a man, and heavy rings of gold are weighed on scales ten feet high while scribes note the amount. The throng of spectators moans with wonder at each new display.

The climax is reached when, one by one, thirty-one

incense trees, with their roots packed in large sacks of soil, are borne ashore. Oh, they are healthy and sturdy and green and beautiful!

As a surprise for me, the Head Porter makes a little speech. Saluting the trees as though they are honored guests, he says, "We bid you welcome, you incense trees, which from love of Makare have departed from your beloved God's Land to come to dwell with her in Amon's realm. Makare will set you in rows before her temple, as her father commanded her to do."

From time to time, one of Nehesi's officers approaches, to bow and present me with a personal gift—an ivory carving, a jar of myrrh ointment, a monkey dressed in a linen tunic and wig. It is all part of the festive occasion.

Now another strides towards me, a gold casket in his hands. His bearing is assured, he smiles, he wears the uniform of an officer, but . . . as he kneels before me he exudes a smell—a smell of *fear*. I sense it as surely as if I were a deer and overhead on a tree limb crouched a leopard.

Before I can speak, my guard takes the extended casket, opens it, extends it toward me. The casket is lined with folded linen, and on it lie two objects. I stare. The guard lifts one out. It is the likeness of a scorpion, exquisitely carved of some brown stone.

All at once casket and scorpion crash together to the ground. The guard cries out, clutching his hand. Across the matting, over my feet, scurries a grotesque creature—a living scorpion, the fat-tailed venomous species, as deadly as a viper. Another guard hastily crushes it under his sandal.

The guard who is bitten is pale with shock and terror. "Majesty, it was in the box . . . along with the other!" He stares in stupefaction at his hand.

The officer who presented the casket is on his feet, running like a hare. Five or six members of my guard dash in pursuit. The man reaches the river, which at present is crowded with craft of all kinds and sizes, their occupants spectators of the fleet's unloading. From boat to boat the man leaps, toward the edge of water where a skiff may await him. My guardsmen are quicker. They seize him in a pandemonium of shouts and shrieks, crashes and splashes. Whatever he knows, which is probably little, will be wrenched from him as the skin from an animal.

My guard with the bitten hand is carried away by two of his fellows.

Senmut leans over me. "Does Her Majesty wish to retire?"

The incident has happened too swiftly to seem more than a scene in a drama. No more than ten persons realize what has taken place.

"Indeed not. I must become inured to danger. Let the unloading proceed."

Lifting my chin, I push the occurrence into a corner of my heart for future study. It will not ruin the most momentous occasion of my reign!

Later, word reaches me that the guard is dead, that his throat closed, his limbs turned blue, he was torn with convulsions. Poor man, he received what was meant for me.

When the last throw stick, the last baboon have left the ship, I rise and address the nobles and courtiers about me. My face and voice are calm, revealing no knowledge of a deliberate attempt at murder.

"While I had to search to the ends of the earth, I at last found what I sought. Amon has his trees, which he commanded me to find. And here I have fashioned for him a garden of Punt, spacious enough for him to walk in."

As the last act of thanksgiving, the High Priest burns incense to Amon and intones a prayer, joined by his assistants. I take a second glance. One of the priests is Thutmose, wearing his usual distant expression. Have I spoiled thy day, my stepson? I will say, thou art a master of disguising thy disappointment. And yet it is possible thou knowest nothing of this attempted killing.

In any case, my happiness is complete. The plot failed because my father Amon proves his love and protects me against all evil. I am the victor over those who hate me. I have demonstrated to the Prince and the priesthood that I am as capable of outstanding achievement as any male ruler; they witness an accomplishment that no other God-King in Egypt's history has equalled . . . that the Prince himself could never equal.

Immediate arrangements will be made. Tomorrow the Prince will become an officer in Egypt's army—

in a distant outpost, on the border with Cush. The garrison is commanded by an elderly cousin of mine, a fierce disciplinarian who bears a grudge toward Lord Rensonb and all of Amon's priests. I will announce to my council that military experience will be of value to my stepson.

"And Rensonb?" Senmut whispers.

My plans for him are also ready. He will be that "conscientious man" needed to restore temple affairs at Hikuptah—Hikuptah, half a country from No-Amon, an entire country from the military post near Cush.

"Your traitorous ideas will languish, Lord Rensonb," I declare to myself, "but perhaps the quiet of Hikuptah will cure your stomach."

Enough of unpleasantness. Tonight there will be a banquet in honor of Lord Nehesi. Later Senmut will help me decide the scenes that will be painted in my House of Eternity, describing the expedition. For this is a grand and magnificent achievement for Great God Amon and for My Majesty, one that will be remembered and remarked on forever and ever.

CHAPTER 15

*Year 12 of the Reign
of His Majesty Makare Hatshepsut*

The morning begins routinely enough. Since for once I have no dispatches to read during my toilet, Henut entertains me.

Her chatter deals mainly with dreams. Henut's sleeping hours appear to be more active than her waking ones; dream succeeds dream. More interesting than the dream itself is its interpretation. At this, Henut is an expert. There is no dream she cannot find a meaning for.

"You are frequently in my dreams, Majesty. Wearing a leopard's head in place of your own."

"What a peculiar fancy."

Eagerly she reassures me. "This signifies you have become a leader, Majesty."

"Are your other dreams so extravagant, Henut?"

She nods. "Nearly so, Majesty. A night or two ago I dreamed of being submerged in the Nile. Can you guess the meaning?" And without waiting for a reply she answers triumphantly, "It is a sign that I have been purged of my sins."

"*Have* you sins, then?" I tease.

She responds seriously, "No longer, Highness. Not after the dream. Also, I dreamed of peering into a well, which signifies being imprisoned. And lo, only a month ago my sister's husband's cousin was arrested for an unpaid debt."

My mind wanders from Henut's innumerable relatives. The first audience of this morning will be with Lord Puyemre, Second Priest of Amon. He has just returned from an inspection tour of Amon's temple in Abydos, convinced that his visits alone keep the temple from tumbling down. I am told he imbues the local priests with fear of me, emphasizing that my spies are everywhere and will report any dereliction in maintenance or ritual. Actually my only so-called spy in Abydos is the High Priest himself, who in turn spins amusing tales of Puyemre.

Today the Second Priest brings me an account of priestly opinion in Abydos.

Henut drones on. "The best omens come from dreams. But one's day of birth is important, too."

"Really?" I ask absently, my mind still on Puyemre.

"Indeed, Majesty. Being born on a certain day sets one's destiny. You have only to consult an almanac.

It tells if one will die of fever or of love or old age, or even inside a crocodile." Henut smacks her lips in grisly enjoyment.

A sudden frown wrinkles her face. "Ah, Majesty! I just remembered. To dream of one's teeth falling out warns of the death of someone near. So I dreamed last night. You must take care, Majesty. There is no arguing with dreams." She speaks with deadly seriousness, regarding me with troubled eyes.

Care. Yes, I take constant care. Besides, if dreams warn, why do they not also suggest the means of countering the warning? This question I keep to myself, as Henut would discourse another hour on the subject. And, at last, my maids can find nothing more in my appearance to improve, and I am ready for the day.

I receive the Second Priest in my new receiving room, a small waiting room that I have redecorated and refurnished. It is now my favorite chamber in the Great House. For one thing, its size is precisely right for two or three people. The young artist who painted it has brought the out of doors inside. The two wooden columns are represented as papyrus stalks, the leaves arching realistically over the turquoise ceiling. With such brightness the room appears light and airy. Around the walls are painted marsh scenes of reeds and flamingos and ducks, and near them the menacing snout of a crocodile.

The furniture of the room consists of a sofa elaborately carved of ebony and piled with bright cushions, two chairs, a few small tables to hold bric-a-brac, and a chest containing boards and men for *senet* and *tjau*, along with scrolls of my favorite poems and stories.

A servant announces the arrival of Puyemre. He is a comical man, his wig always too large, so that inside it his head slides as easily as an eye in its socket. Before each utterance he takes a deep breath and blinks his eyes rapidly five or six times, as though about to dive into the river.

"So, Lord Puyemre." I motion him from his knees. "The news from the temple in Abydos is good?"

But no, it is not. I can tell from the extra blinks and the *two* deep breaths.

"Your Majesty, it is my duty to speak the truth." His Adam's apple bobs nervously. Oh, surely the news is bad.

"Certainly. And mine to hear it."

"Ummm, ummm. Has Your Majesty ever contemplated the reworking of those old gold mines in the eastern desert, those near the Wady. . .?"

"I have not. Come to the point, Puyemre."

His wig slips over one cheek, giving him a tipsy air. "Majesty, I speak only that His Majesty may be aware of the gossip, as His Majesty has bade me do."

What mishap can have befallen? "Speak at once."

"Majesty, it is said that without foreign conquest gold grows scarce in the Two Lands. That the golden vessels of the Great Temple must soon be replaced with copper. That the veins of gold in the mines dwin-

173

dle to nothing." He pants, out of words and breath.

So. They speak thus even in Abydos.

"What stupidity. No gold for Amon, indeed! Every month I present vessels and shrines and statues of gold to Amon throughout Upper and Lower Egypt."

"They say those vessels are of gilded copper."

"Who are *they*?"

Twenty blinks. "The priests hint such things to the people. The rumors spread as the Nile does in flood. I contradict when I can."

"You do well, Second Priest. I wish to be informed of all such gossip."

There is plenty of gold in Egypt. But the priesthood grows in size and power and greed. Unwilling to contain its avarice, it spreads its vicious reports. Now it has decided war is the answer, war to bring in land and slaves and booty and tribute to stuff Amon's coffers. As a female ruler cannot lead Egypt's troops in conquest, I am expected to renounce my throne—in favor, of course, of Thutmose.

My stepson has made himself a reputation at his isolated military post. At the first hint of local trouble, he is away with his men, eager to quell any uprising. It appears the Prince has at last found his calling: He is a born soldier. I will say, our border with Cush is as secure as it has ever been.

Puyemre bows his way out, and I call for Senmut. What would I ever do without my Unique Friend, with whom I discuss every problem? He is more necessary to me than any or all of my limbs, his mind equals mine—nearly. Or rather, the one complements the other. Together, I feel, Senmut and I possess the might of the sun and the moon.

"Majesty?" Senmut is considerately formal always, in front of others.

I dismiss my attendants and relate to him Puyemre's report. "The Second Priest mentioned something that might be of use. The eastern gold mines, those abandoned but not yet exhausted, could be reworked."

Senmut nods thoughtfully. "Abandoned for a reason. There are few wells in that region. Water must be stored in gigantic jars buried along the road. To replenish it requires tremendous effort."

"I know. And miners are as difficult to find as water. Under the insufferable conditions of the desert, no one volunteers."

Senmut shrugs. "There is a sufficiency of convicts and foreign captives for the work, I suppose."

"Yes. But it seems they quickly sicken and die. As much from hopelessness as disease."

Senmut smiles at me. "Thou must command Prince Thutmose to send some of his Cush rebels to thy mines."

We reach no solution, but Senmut succeeds as usual in lightening my problems and putting them in perspective. We will think more on the matter. By wresting gold from those mines, I could effectively silence the carping priests.

My Vizier has requested the second audience of the day for a special reason. None but Pharaoh can prescribe capital punishment for a felony, and today a prisoner pleads his case in the crime of crimes. I know already what sentence I shall pronounce, but the wretch's story may be enlightening. Moreover, because the priests are ever eager for me to exhibit weakness, I shall make a point of viewing the ordeal with no womanly queasiness and with all the toughness of a man. No one will ever say of me, "She bore the title of a king but the heart of a woman."

Two guards drag in the prisoner, thrust him down before me. He is a small, sinewy man with long and narrow eyes; these burn with sullenness and no sign of repentance for his horrendous sin against the dead.

Hapusoneb questions the kneeling man. "Your name?"

"Djaou."

"Djaou, *Your Majesty.*" Hapusoneb glares, and a guard kicks the prisoner. His feet are bruised and bloody from beatings.

"Two days ago you were caught in the act of robbing the tomb of Lord Rekht, Chancellor of the Good God Pharoah Amenhotep. You confess this?"

The man mumbles faintly.

"What induced you to commit the crime? Knowing it to be an act against the state as well as the gods, in particular against Osiris?"

The prisoner has the effrontery to shrug. "I worship Set, not Osiris."

"Set, god of the desert, brother and murderer of Osiris! A fitting god for a thief." Hapusoneb's face is crimson with indignation. "Set cannot admit you to the Underworld."

Another mumble.

"Speak up!"

"I hold no belief in Osiris or the Underworld."

Hapusoneb gasps at this impiety. "Ignorant wretch. As well for you then, since you have no hope of entering it. You should at least feel some shame for your act. By robbing Lord Rekht you deprive *him* of the comforts of the Hereafter."

I interrupt. "Did he harm in any way the bodies of Lord Rekht or his wife?"

"No, Your Highness. Although doubtless that was his intent . . . his and his companion's intent. They were too swiftly apprehended to damage the mummies."

I motion for a cushion to be placed behind my back. "Let him recount his story."

The prisoner's eyes have lost their luster. He appears pitiful and dejected. A guard shoves him, and he coughs and licks his lips.

"Give him water."

A guard holds a bowl to the man's mouth, and in two huge swallows he has emptied it. Wearily he raises his head.

"Quickly! His Majesty waits!" Hapusoneb, that master of efficiency, tolerates sluggishness in no one.

The prisoner sighs and speaks abruptly. "We took a walk. In the valley there. For no reason, only to pass the time."

"Why should you walk there among the homes of the dead? Far from your own home? Who is *we*?"

"Four of us. Hod, my friend, who is now dead. Two others. Our work was to excavate tombs in the rock of that area. The workmen's camp is close by."

"So that is how you knew the location of Lord Rekht's Eternal Home?"

"We did not know it. We watched the cliff as we walked. I spied a small hole, like an animal's lair. We climbed up there. I dropped a pebble into the hole, carefully, in case it housed a snake. The pebble fell a long distance before it hit the bottom. It had to be a shaft. We smashed open the hole. My friends lowered me on a rope."

Hapusoneb shakes his head. "Innocent men would not be carrying ropes on a walk. So what did you find?"

"I crawled over rubble and into a chamber. It was black dark and I could only feel my way. I felt a chair, finely carved, then a stool, then more furniture. Large objects which I could not identify. Then a narrow doorway. It led into another chamber, where lay a great mass of carved stone. The sarcophagus, I thought. There were more rooms, but I turned back—"

"Taking along a cedar-and-ebony chest containing jewelry of the lord Rekht."

"I did not know what it contained. My friends drew me up." The man's head droops.

"The four of you examined the jewelry and made your plans."

The prisoner stares defiantly at the Vizier. "We intended no harm to the lord. The loss of a few jewels . . . that could not have hurt him. . . . They would have fed my family for a year."

"Stop your impudence, fellow! You and Hod schemed to rid yourselves of your two companions. How?"

"We returned home. Later that night we took Hod's son—he is eight years—to the hole. We lowered him with food and water. When early the next morning the two others returned with us to the hole, the boy moaned and shrieked. Our companions believed there were *sheftis,* spirits, there. Ay! They ran howling. . . ." He almost smiles at the memory.

"Then you and Hod robbed the tomb at your leisure."

"Only the jewels. And two gold vessels."

"*Four* gold vessels. No more for one reason: The tomb guards glimpsed the flicker of your candles and captured you."

The man's face sags. For another crime I might have pitied him. But to rob the dead? Perhaps to burn corpses so that the victim's *ka* will not take revenge? The destruction of the body signifies the second and final murder of the soul. Without a body there can be no Hereafter.

With the ruthlessness of a male pharaoh I pronounce judgment. "For crimes against society, against the gods, My Majesty sentences you to execution. Your body will be thrown into the river."

The guards remove the prisoner. I push the depressing scene from my mind and offer the Vizier a goblet of wine.

As I sip mine, I bring up Puyemre's suggestion of opening the eastern gold mines. "Unfortunately, that area is unfit for human habitation," I remark.

"Is it possible the Overseer of the Administrative Office of the Mansion could suggest a remedy?"

There is no hint of sarcasm in Hapusoneb's voice or manner, although I know it is there. I will not reprimand him. He refers to Lord Senmut's most recent title.

Senmut has long since been recognized as my favored counselor, but still some of my courtiers are jealous. True, I have heaped offices on him, for he fulfills them admirably. And if he boasts of his titles, why not? He deserves them. I am told other officials find him intolerable. To me he is the most useful and sympathetic of advisers, my Beloved Companion, who has never attempted to dominate me in any way. He is wise, for no man will ever dominate Hatshepsut.

"Perhaps he can," I reply coolly.

To that Hapusoneb is silent. I think with compunction that he is a capable and loyal vizier and should be treated well.

"Come, Lord, take time from your work and play me a game of *tjau*," I say.

This is perhaps not a kindness to him after all, since his duties are numerous and his schedule will be delayed. But I have a new board of onyx and ivory, just completed by one of the temple craftsmen, and men carved with animal heads of jade and jasper.

"With pleasure, Your Majesty." Vizier's manners are impeccable. He even manages to look pleased.

I play the game only with Hapusoneb and Senmut. Both are better at it than I, but at least I can tell when they allow me to win. Sometimes I can truly beat them. A good match could be had between the two of them, Hapusoneb so steady and farseeing, Senmut more impatient, but with flashes of brilliance.

The board, set into a folding table, is brought, along with wine and a dish of pomegranates. Just as I seat myself, Henut bursts into the room, her eyes wild.

CHAPTER 16

"Majesty . . ." She gasps for breath and for the first time in her life neglects to bow.

A terrible chill catches my heart. "Senmut?"

"The princess Nefrure." Tears roll down her cheeks. "The dream . . . my dream of teeth . . . it was to warn me of this evil. . . . Why did I not heed . . . ?"

I seize her arm. "What is it, what has happened to Nefrure?"

"A snake, Majesty." She wrings her hands. "In the garden. The Princess bent to pick a flower. The viper was coiled just there in the shadow—so small it was. The girl Ani attending the Princess saw the head dart forward and back, once or twice or more, too swiftly to count. . . ."

"Take me to her."

I yank up my long tight skirt that I may run. Henut,

with her curved back, seems to move no faster than a tortoise.

"The doctor Khun has been summoned?"

"Majesty, four doctors there are with her, and I have sent for priests and potions and amulets and scrolls and—"

"Hurry! Does she lie in her room?"

"Yes, Highness."

I fly down the corridors, the guards agog. Vizier's footsteps echo my own. Into my daughter's room, jammed with people of all ranks, I dash. The people sink to their knees.

Oh, my Nefrure! There are dark circles about her eyes. The eyes themselves are wells of pain. Her breathing is rapid and harsh, her whole body quivering with the effort to draw in air.

One of the physicians steps forward and waves a flat curving wand carved with magical symbols over Nefrure's convulsive body. The wand is made of a hippopotamus tusk and is much famed as a protection against snakebite.

I snatch it and hurl it into a corner. "It is too late for that! You must exorcise the snake demons!"

The doctors shake with terror. In despair I realize they are as impotent as I against the catastrophe.

Two high priests enter the chamber, one swinging a censer of incense, the other unrolling a wide scroll. They bow to me gravely, make their way to the bed. Incantations against snakebite, against disease in general, against evil, roll through the room, the rhythmic gleam of the waving censer nearly hypnotizing me.

But Nefrure's spasms grow worse, and she chokes from the fumes of the incense. Two more priests arrive, scrolls clutched to their breasts.

From a corner of the room, where he has been working with bowls and jars of ill-smelling mashes, there pushes a tall, balding man. He is Dr. Khun, the chief palace physician. He carries a golden dish of some slimy concoction.

"What is that?" I ask.

"Blood of lizard, dung of cat, powdered poppy root, a most effective remedy . . . against some snakebite."

The last words are terrifying. They are an excuse for failure. My daughter is dying, and these men have no power in medicine or magic to cure her. I, who am pharaoh, have no power either. Who has?

My divine father Amon, to whom I have raised obelisks and repaired temples and am now constructing the most splendid mortuary temple in the world— he must help me.

I tear from the room, ripping my skirt as I run. To my own chapel I speed, and fall to my knees before the altar.

"My sacred father, for thy daughter's sake, heal my child! I promise thee more gold than twenty donkeys can carry, I promise thee land and fields of grain, monuments, temples, half the tribute paid to Egypt . . ."

I am beside myself with grief and desperation. I knock my head to the cold brick floor again and again until I am nearly senseless.

The golden image of Amon residing on its ebony throne makes no response to my frenzied pleas.

"My father, thou didst create me to rule Egypt for thee! If I am left with no child, who will rule after me? Who will serve thee as fully as I?"

Still Amon stares, without word or movement.

Worn out, I drag myself to my feet, totter out through the antechamber. On the other side of the heavy linen hanging Henut waits, her face screwed into a wet rag.

"She is gone. Oh, Majesty, she is gone!" She breaks into cracked wails.

I fly to my daughter's room. She lies still and white as a statue. The lighthearted butterfly whom the world loved is no more. Senmut kneels beside her, groaning and weeping, his tears splotching the floor.

But Pharaoh shall not weep. How can I weep, when my daughter will soon play in the fields of Ialu?

From long habit I speak in a calm flat voice. "We must prepare her for eternity. Henut, we must see that she has everything to make her happy there."

Inside my cold mask I am wrung and knotted with anguish. Life stretches before me dim and gray, like the morning mists on the delta, without the bright color of Nefrure's laughter.

The news is posted throughout the kingdom. "The Princess is dead. The Residence is hushed, hearts are in mourning, the Great Gates are closed, the courtiers crouch head on lap, and the nobles grieve."

During the period of mourning I think more of my daughter than I did while she lived. Not that I did not love her—I adored her—but I took her for granted. I realize that now.

Through her our line was to continue to reign. Not through the Prince, that presumptuous upstart—but through the son of some high noble. On that score I was biding my time, with no sense of urgency, waiting for the proper youth, the proper moment. Their son could have followed me in office. Now that will never be.

Henut quavers, "The blame can be cast on no one." But she faults herself, berates herself for not heeding her dream of loose teeth, for not shadowing my daughter.

And I wonder. Perhaps I was negligent in the amulets she wore. An Eye-of-Horus or a thrice-knotted anklet would have offered her more protection. Or was Amon, ruffled by my pride and my overconfidence, determined to bring me down? Perhaps he has turned against me; the gods are ever inconstant and capricious.

Or did the priests, because of the sacrilege of the destroyed temple roof, because of their frustration at a female ruler, employ magic for their revenge? My fancies twist and weave together like a sand swirl, with no beginning or end.

My only consolation comes from my Dear Friend. Yet in this adversity he is weaker than I. Senmut, whose tenderest nature was always directed toward Nefrure, is sadly afflicted, though tempered by his confidence in the Hereafter.

"She was young and virtuous. She will have no need of spells written in her tomb to be assured of Eternity. Her heart is too light with innocence to outweigh the feather of Truth."

He tells me that once he had begged of Nefrure a sheet marked with her name as a burial sheet for his father. For him Nefrure had added a ring, saying, "My lord Senmut, this will truly ensure thy father of Osiris's protection, for it has been blessed at the temple of Abydos." At the memory Senmut breaks into sobs.

I cannot weep. My pain weighs like stone, encasing my heart.

The Princess's tomb will lack for nothing. The priesthood has been paid for food offerings daily for twenty years. We will include her childhood toys and pastimes, the ivory palette still mounded with colors, her sistrum, the crocodile whose jaws snap at the pull of a string, the dolls of gazelle skin, and her favorite flat wooden one with its long beaded plaits of hair. Often I listened as Nefrure raced through the garden, her doll in her arms, its beaded braids clattering against the wood. Now the Great House is drear and somber, cloaked in a gloom I could never have imagined.

How much my sunny Nefrure laughed, and how much I miss the sound. The painted representations of ourselves in our Houses of Eternity do not portray laughter, rather a certain grimness. For that reason I order two hundred *shabtis*, pottery figures, for my daughter's tomb, all featured with radiant smiles. They will keep her cheerful company, and at her call will answer happily, "Here am I!"

To occupy my listless mind I deliberate on the furnishings of her last home. Her little chair, of course, a copy of my lion-footed throne but smaller. Dishes of pomegranates and date cakes, which she could never have enough of. A memory intrudes.

When she was very small, Nefrure would help herself to cakes at palace banquets, folding five or six in a linen scarf.

"So many cakes, my daughter!" I would chide. "I believe thou art greedy."

"But no, my mother," she would protest. "Some are for my doll Toli and some are for Mu, my kitten."

"Does Mu like cakes?"

"Not much, but Toli does."

I could not help but laugh . . . then.

During this terrible time I must force my mind to face the problems that still exist. The priests, I am told, hint that the Princess's death is Amon's punishment for my making myself king. Against a consuming apathy I call for the High Priest and for Senmut.

To needle the High Priest, a smug, narrow-minded old man who never admits anyone is right except himself, I seat Senmut beside me and have High Priest stand before us.

"My Majesty has heard absurd rumors, which appear to originate in the temple."

High Priest jerks his chin upward. "Rumors, Majesty?" He plays the innocent.

"That My Majesty neglects his duties of office. That Amon is displeased with his daughter. What foolishment! My Majesty's government performs smoothly, as always."

The High Priest presses his lips together into two thin worms. "Amon's priest understands, Majesty, that this calamity occurs as a warning from the God of Gods."

"My daughter's death a warning! You suggest, then, that were Amon content with his subjects, he would allow them to live forever?"

High Priest twists his lips. He is certain my argument is one of female illogic, but he is not logical enough himself to detect the flaw. "The death of the Princess is a particular case," he begins heavily.

"The opinion that death is punishment is witless. Everyone dies. In time even you, Lord, will face Great God Osiris. Let us hope your heart will not fail the test. For now, My Majesty desires the baseless rumors to cease." My eyes bore fiery holes into High Priest's skull.

The man bows and, with his mouth now a jagged crack, backs clumsily through the door.

I look at Senmut and sigh. "To defy the priesthood is to grasp a handful of smoke. It will never admit to wrongdoing."

My Friend sends me a look of affection. "Thou art ever courageous, Hatshepsut. Thou never avoidst a confrontation. That in itself confounds the priesthood. The High Priest will henceforth curtail the rumors."

"But not stop them completely."

"Thou wishest for the fields of Ialu here on earth."

Ah, Senmut is a comfort to me. Yes, for the moment the rumors may desist. And my strength will return. It *must* return.

At last the seventy days of mourning, of silence and weeping and fasting throughout the land, are over. It is the morning of the funeral. The turquoise bowl fits over us, and Amon's chariot has begun its day's journey.

I endure the rituals of prayer, which seem today insufferably long, the further tedious ritual of being groomed for the ceremony. None of my attendants speaks. Like me they have become dull and apathetic. Only Henut charges about, fussing here, scolding there, recognizing that life stops for no one, not even a princess.

I wish she would chide *me* into action. The priesthood with its vicious lies seeks like a deadly miasma to suffocate me. Can Thutmose be behind this, or is he merely a willing pawn?

The troublemongers among the priests are well disguised. Their solemn faces are no clue to the workings in their heads. At the moment my mind is numb. I feel crushed and trampled, like those Asiatics defeated by my father and pictured in his tomb as writhing worms.

I am ready. The inevitable cosmetics have been left off for once. To honor my daughter I wear Pharaoh's full regalia. Resolution seeps slowly through me: I will see to it that this is a splendid funeral, one to surpass all funerals, to be remembered always.

Flanked by the High Priest and the Vizier, I walk with slow tread to the dock, following the sledge, drawn by four oxen, that bears Nefrure's coffins. These are beautiful. Nefrure would have been—will be—proud of them. The one enclosing her body is of beaten gold; it is set, along with tens of magical scarabs and scrolls, in a coffin of gold inlaid with gems. These two lie in a chest of fine cedar beautifully painted with intricate designs in gilt, blue, and crimson, centered here and there about the Eye-of-Horus.

After follows a line of servants bearing a garden of flowers, furniture enough to equip a palace, chests of clothing, sunshades, fans, jewelry, dishes. Nefrure must want for nothing.

Behind the servants straggles the court: government officials and nobles and politicians, foreign envoys and businessmen, all strung out in mournful procession. In contrast to their usual smartness, the women are bare of ornament and makeup, and many have rubbed dirt into their clothing and hair.

The multitude of professional mourners surrounding us outdoes itself in shrieks and howls and groans. They scrabble on the ground, pour handfuls of sand and dust over their heads, claw their skin into bloody ridges, work themselves into a state of hysteria. Nefrure would have been horrified by the wild eyes and cries; she was a sedate child.

At the river they seat me beside the coffins in the

191

main funeral vessel, its high prow and stern carved to represent a papyrus plant. The Vizier drops into a seat behind me; he pants and coughs and tries to subdue both. Exposure to the fiery heat will do him little good, although the canopy shades him from the worst of the sun. Beside him the High Priest adjusts his cape of leopard skin.

In a nearby boat I glimpse the Prince, returned from the garrison for the funeral. Bitterly I have wondered, Why could not the viper have bitten *him* instead of my Nefrure? It cannot be that Amon forsakes me and now favors the Prince. And yet . . . the signs are there. A tremor of panic shakes my mind. Can it be that my destiny, like a long, smooth-flowing river, has broken into rapids and muddy turbulence? Resolution, Hatshepsut!

But the Prince preys on my thoughts. Of what does he think? That one of his roads to the throne has vanished? His power grows, and with my daughter's death he now poses more and more a fierce threat to me. What will his next move be? At this instant I do not care. If I could exchange my crown for Nefrure's life, I would do so.

Wouldst thou indeed, Hatshepsut? my heart whispers. No. Thou wouldst not. Moreover, thou canst not—the deed is done. Now thou must fight to defend thyself and thy throne. Henceforth the battle will be more grim, more deadly, without the presence of the Princess to soften it. Henceforth there will be no one to share thy heart except Senmut.

I lift my head imperiously. "Why are we waiting?"

There is always a delay for one reason or another. The other boats are filling with courtiers, fearful that the pecking order of protocol will be unobserved and they will find themselves either far outranked or, worse, far outranking.

The gong sounds, the dirge commences, the oarsmen dip their oars in time to it. Our vessel, towed by two others, glides slowly through the water. We leave the bank thronged with grieving spectators.

The western bank is as crowded as the eastern. The eyes of the people are for once not directed at me but toward the coffins.

"Eternal life to the Princess!"

"A quick passage to the fields of Ialu!"

"Pray for us, guard us, little Princess!"

Flowers, amulets, good-luck charms, are tossed at the coffins. My people feel and express more affection toward a child than they do toward Pharaoh. Their love is pure, unmixed with reverence or respect or fear.

Awaiting me on the wharf is Senmut, who has supervised the last-minute arrangements at the tomb. He bows deeply, helps me from the boat. More than anyone else he has grieved for Nefrure. More than anyone save myself she loved him. Often arrogant and pompous to others (as a defense, I believe, for being lowborn), he was always gentle and cheerful, even playful, with her.

The coffins are loaded onto another sledge, which

is hauled up the long, rough, stony path to the rock tomb cut into the valley cliffs. Wearily we trudge behind.

Senmut whispers, "The carrying-chair is near. It can carry thee."

I shake my head. A god-king's mortality must at times be suppressed.

By the time we reach my daughter's House of Eternity, I appear all too mortal. Perspiration drenches my tunic, my face is streaked with dust, my neck aches with supporting the heavy crown. Henut and the serving women circle about me, dry my face.

We enter the long passage, behind the coffins borne by six priests. Only a few officials and priests, Senmut, Henut, and I assemble in the main chamber next to the small room where Nefrure will lie forever.

As the High Priest intones the service, I glance about at the walls that glow with color in the flickering lamplight. There are scenes of Nefrure being blessed by the goddesses Mut, Isis, and Hathor. In another scene my daughter stands before the Great God Osiris while jackal-headed Anubis weighs her heart on the great scale against the feather of Truth. Beside him waits the monster to devour anyone whose heart outweighs the feather. Nefrure is in no peril from *him*.

Around the walls my daughter is pictured as making the journey to the Underworld, past demons and spirits and unnatural animals, across a wide river to reach the fields of Ialu, calm and peaceful, teeming with fields of grain and orchards.

194

The room is crowded with her bed, chairs, tables, sofas, her toys and games, wooden models of the cooks preparing her date cakes and other sweets, another of a bathroom, that she may be clean and fresh always. On top of chests and coffers lie an ornate carrying-chair and a boat with an embroidered awning for pleasure excursions. The heaps of smiling *shabtis* appear eager to begin serving their mistress.

The service concluded, the High Priest enters the burial room, where Nefrure's coffins are propped upright against a wall. He touches the sacred chisel to the mouth of the mask, to the eyes, nose, and ears, muttering the magic charm. With the "Opening of the Mouth" Nefrure's spirit is released to take up her interrupted life, to flutter about her accustomed haunts, to commence her journey to the serene fields.

And, I think, this man, the High Priest, who functions so well in freeing my daughter's spirit, is my enemy. With joy he would send *my* spirit to the fields, and here on earth he will oppose me with all his strength. Very well, Lord, we will see who enters the fields first, you or I. Resolution, Hatshepsut!

At the end of the ceremony all gather before the tomb for the funeral feast. The melancholy songs of the harpers beat on my ears.

"Desist, musicians! Rather, play a merry tune for my daughter, she would much prefer that" is what I long to cry. As Pharaoh I stifle my impulses. At least when I follow tradition I am spared having to think.

Farewell, my daughter, until I join thee in the beautiful fields. Henceforth no one will know—except Senmut—how much I miss thee. The scar over my wound will be so thick and hard and tough that no weapon can ever pierce it.

Now, Hatshepsut, back to the battle of life.

CHAPTER 17

*Year 16 of the Reign
of His Majesty Makare Hatshepsut*

The morning begins with a conference with Senmut. For four years we have worked on a plan to reopen the old gold mines in the eastern desert. The obstacles, the complications, have seemed at times insurmountable. But to me no impediment is insurmountable; it is only challenging.

"The project is nearly at an end," I remark. "Art thou as relieved as I?"

Senmut smiles. "It has been a game—a pleasant, exciting game—played by the two of us. Why should I wish it to end?"

I shake my head. "There remain games without limit ahead of us. This one I tire of. The final well has been dug?"

My Sole Companion dons his business face. "The wells are dug. The stations between the wells have been settled, the routine of bringing in water and food established, even small gardens planted."

"And the priesthood swore I could not do it! Once gold begins to flow into No-Amon, I will rub their holy noses in it."

"Certainly this should stop their grumblings that Amon's coffers are as empty as the Nile's bed just before inundation. With more gold in circulation, the priesthood should cease its urgings toward conquest and tribute."

"The priests resemble a flock of crows that takes delight in pecking at one of their number. They are bullies and cowards."

Senmut makes no reply. He half agrees with me, half fears and reveres the priests. I neither fear nor revere. The priesthood is necessary to Egypt, and I accept it. My Friend leaves me, and I muse for a time.

For four years now my daughter has resided in the fields of Ialu. During many, many nights—the sole time I am alone and can think my long thoughts—I have remembered her and wondered for what reason Amon took her from me.

A loving father does not snatch away his daughter's dearest treasure for no reason. And Amon loves me above all others. Gods are easily offended: for lack of respect, for lack of offerings, for lack of reverence. I have erred in none of these. The death of my brothers, my father, my husband, all resulted in my ascending to the throne, a proof of Amon's love. But Nefrure's death puzzles me.

Occasional strange fancies trouble me. What if, because I made myself king, Amon punishes me? No. The idea is sick, for the gods care nothing for our actions—except those that concern themselves. To follow *maat*—to preserve order, serenity, tradition in our lives—has been Egypt's creed since history began. It is my creed as well.

I refuse to believe rumors that Thutmose, now a high officer in the military who comes and goes as he pleases, has formed a pact with Amon: In exchange for the god's aid to make him ruler of the Two Lands, he will spread the worship of Amon throughout the world.

Nonsense. Amon will never abandon me for my stepson. He will not turn against his favored daughter, who loves and honors him. And yet . . . and yet . . . the thought chills me. After what happened two days ago I begin to wonder, almost to doubt Amon's love.

We were on the river for a pleasure cruise, Senmut and I, with our attendants. A papyrus skiff passed us, holding three men, each armed with a long spear.

Senmut gave a lazy laugh. "They have been hunting hippopotamus. That is the sort of spear used, one with a rope attached. When the animal sinks to the bottom of the river after being wounded, it can be hauled out by the rope, noosed, and killed."

"This is not the region for hippopotamus," I objected.

Our eyes followed the skiff. Just beyond us the rower stopped his paddling. The men all stared intently into the water. Did they spy a great fish, a crocodile? Our boat drew abreast. Senmut and I leaned out, eying them with interest. The spearmen were foreign; they wore the black beards of Syrians and were gaunt and ill-favored. Suddenly turning to face us, they jabbered in a strange tongue; their eyes burned. One pointed toward me, lifted his spear.

Then I was rudely pushed from my chair. I lay dazed on the deck. Senmut was beside me, holding a heavy shield over me. What was happening?

Our guards were shouting and hurling spears. My shrieking maids were huddled over me. Senmut sat up, his arm bloody. Splashing, howls, and commotion rent the peace of the river.

"They meant to kill His Majesty!" cried my little maid.

The danger appeared to be over, and I regained my composure. Senmut helped me to my chair. I was bruised and scratched, otherwise unharmed. My Sole Companion had a small cut.

"Bring them before me," I commanded my Chief of Guard.

"Majesty, they are dead. Two in the river, drowned. The third has stabbed himself."

"We will never know the author of the plot!" I exclaimed. But of course I knew.

In a tiny space of time the episode was over, the attempt foiled, the assassins dead. Had not my Unique Friend been alert, I should myself have been dead and

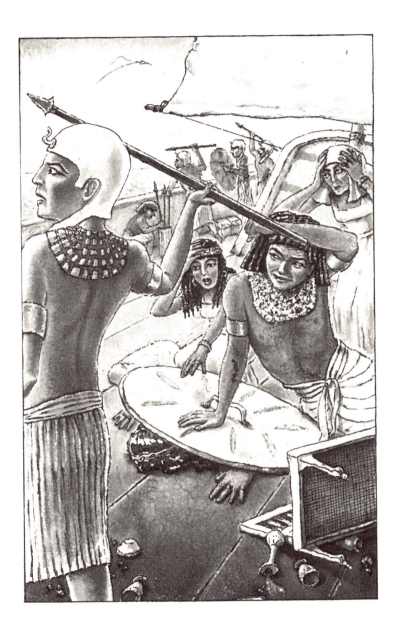

the Prince have gained his purpose. Whether he planned the event or someone else, the objective was the same: for the Prince to take my place on Egypt's throne.

Fury swept through me. My enemies would use any means to rid themselves of me—a venomous scorpion, three venomous and miserable foreigners. Why would the Prince not face me himself, challenge me to mortal combat? Athletic as he is, he would not down me without feeling my claws!

By the time we reached home, my anger threatened to burst my body asunder. I quivered and trembled and panted with it inwardly. But my voice was cool, my face impassive, when I summoned my Chief of Guard.

"You will collect one hundred Syrians from No-Amon and execute them," I command. "Before the public execution you will read out a proclamation stating *why* they are to die." No one attempts Pharaoh's life lightly.

The Chief of Guard sent me an uncertain glance and I read his thoughts. "If Syria resents the act, we will inform her ambassador that I resent assassins," I said dryly.

"At once, Your Majesty."

The man left and I brooded. Why should Thutmose resent me so? Nay, more. I was told his resentment had now turned to bitter hatred, that he considered me the barrier to his own rule.

Why? Why *should* he? I governed as well as any

pharaoh in history. He would have his turn. True, I could not lead the army to the end of the world, but there was no reason for that. No nation threatened the Two Lands. The truth was the Prince wasted too much time in mulling over fancied wrongs, and the narrow-minded priesthood sulked for a male king.

Henut asked, "Does not the attempt on your life leave Your Majesty atremble?"

Never. But it frustrated me, infuriated me, for there was no action I could take.

"Why dost thou not serve the Prince as he serves thee?" Senmut wished to know.

Prepare an accident, a mishap for my stepson? Justice would perhaps be served—but not *maat*. It was a course of action I could not persuade myself to. Father would have considered the act shameful.

"Assassination is cowardly," he used to say with contempt. "Confront thine enemy face to face—not from behind."

Enough of dark thoughts. I have a more agreeable subject to dwell on.

The *zesru zeser*, my mortuary temple, is nearly complete. Just installed are the great doors of black bronze with their inlaid figures of electrum, like moonbeams against the dark of night. The edifice is the most splendid in the Two Lands, in the entire world.

Senmut's conceit of setting twenty-six statues of Osiris, the heads carved with my face, to border the third and topmost courtyard, has been carried out with success. The temple rises in three tiers of extensive courtyards and colonnaded porticos. The lowest courtyard, decorated with sphinxes bearing my head alternating with the series of myrrh trees of Punt, truly is like to a garden of the gods.

At midday in the strong sunlight the structure gleams white against the heavy yellow cliffs. But at dawn and at sunset, when the cliffs grow rose with the low sun, my temple is tinted a faint pink, like a pearl of Keftiu. One feels like crying out, "That is surely the dwelling place of Amon himself!" If for nothing else, I will be forever remembered for this monument.

Only one disappointment rises from my temple. I had wished a tomb chamber for myself excavated in the royal valley, with an entranceway tunneled through the mountain to this, Amon's holy-of-holies. Sadly, after many attempts, the mountain refuses to be cleft. Even Senmut dissuades me from trying yet again.

"The cliff behind the sublime-of-sublimes may dissolve, like a fallen curtain," he tells me. "I have wished this as much as thou, but I am convinced it is impossible."

So be it. My Hereditary Prince and Count has done his utmost. This afternoon we go together for the hundredth time, or perhaps the thousandth, to inspect my temple in West-of-the-City.

Senmut is a curious mixture of genius, sophistication, and superstition. The first two traits I am proud to have nurtured; the third I can do nothing to root out.

After a period of silence on his part, he speaks abruptly. "I am assured, Majesty, that the lower a man's birth, the more help he needs to attain the Hereafter."

I shrug. It may be so. Sometimes I have uneasy fancies that even the highest born may require more than scrolls and amulets and magic, however potent, to assist them past the horrors of the Underworld's entrance.

"Indeed?"

He nods hesitantly. "My most fervent hope is to serve Her Majesty in the Afterlife. I would do all possible to achieve that end." These words are spoken with a peculiar earnestness.

"I am certain thou wilt serve me," I reassure him. "Have I not provided for thy tomb chamber to be carved under my very temple? Have I not furnished it to honor thee above all mortals? Unless thy heart be laden with sin, thou canst not help but join me in the land of Osiris." I smile with my pleasantry in hopes it will relieve his mind.

Still he seems troubled and perplexed.

Impatiently I change the subject. "Regard this scene of the loading of vessels at Punt. Is not the panther well executed?"

He replies automatically but does not return to the matter that appears to gnaw at his heart as a rat gnaws at bread. Perhaps with age his thoughts tend toward morbidity.

For Senmut has aged. From the lean and lively and

blithe man I first knew, he has grown paunchy and smooth and complacent with prosperity. That, too, I take to my credit, for I have been the cause of his success. I might say we have been successful together. Yet with the death of Nefrure our joint success perhaps has turned hard, the way leather, denied oil and loving care, grows stiff and inflexible.

Certainly today Senmut's ruminations do run to the morose. "There is talk, Majesty, that Egypt's neighbors to the east wax restless."

"Such talk goes on constantly."

"Hmm, hmm, yes. Still, fear of another invasion of the Two Lands increases. A mighty invasion, like that of the Hyksos before the time of thy great-grandfather."

"That is absurd. When those vagabonds invaded, Egypt was divided and indecisive. Today she is neither. It is an insult to my rule that thou takest notice of such gossip."

"I speak of it to warn thee." Senmut's tone is lugubrious. Really, today he is tiresome. "There is talk in the army that an attack should be made against Egypt's neighbors—before they think to make war on *us*. The man favored to lead the attack is the Prince."

Senmut is the being closest to my heart. I have full confidence in his sincerity and loyalty. But he has ever viewed my stepson as a threat, a kind of monster similar to the Devourer of the Underworld, waiting to pounce on the unready.

His overconcern lessens my own concern about Thutmose. How could this boy (man really, although to me he is still no more than a youth) make a move of any sort without the hawkish eye of Senmut or my "Eyes and Ears" discerning it?

"That might be a satisfactory way to employ his talents," I remark lightly.

Of course I am not serious. With his energy and determination (at his age I had the same or more), Thutmose would end by conquering half of Asia and returning home a hero. That would not in the least suit my plans. There is room for only one sun in the heavens.

My Unique Friend shakes his head and persists in his melancholy. "The Prince gathers prestige in the army. He is looked on as a worthy grandson to Her Majesty's father."

I have seldom heard Senmut so crabbed, as sour as an unripe grape. He is ruining my visit to my *zesru zeser*.

"Let us speak no further of this," I say sharply. "The Prince is an army officer, no more. May he impress the other officers with his high-flown words. They cannot harm me. I am Amon's beloved daughter."

For the present we bury the subject—not, unfortunately, in the sands at our feet, but in our hearts, where it is too easily unearthed.

Climbing to the highest level of my temple, I look

down over the wide courtyards to the green fields divided by the river. To myself I whisper, "Hapi, god of the Nile, Egypt would be nothing without thee." I picture to myself a land abandoned by Hapi to Set, all red sand and rock and brooding desert, a dead country. The Black Land is truly blessed.

CHAPTER 18

Disturbing news draws to itself further dread news, as a flock of ducks floating on a pond will lure other ducks from the air. As I sit in my chamber at breakfast a few days later, a servant enters.

"The lord Hapusoneb waits, O Majesty. He entreats an immediate audience with His Majesty."

Bother. Can I not have my meals in peace? The Vizier has already two audiences scheduled with me today.

Well, it is the price of being Pharaoh. "Admit him," I order with resignation.

Unlike Senmut, Hapusoneb with age has become more spare, more wrinkled, his clothing more disarrayed. His hair, which escapes his wig as a fern overflows a pot, is white at the roots, where he has neglected to dye it.

He bows low, his face all drooping: mouth, cheeks, jowls; even the nose is curled downward. I motion him to sit, signal a servant to set a table before him with wine and cakes.

My Vizier fusses with a cake, fails to utter the inconsequential remarks leading up to the gist of an audience. My appetite dwindles to nothing.

Finally he removes the table and stands. "An unspeakable act of sacrilege has been committed, Your Highness." His voice trembles, and his old eyes, focused as they always are to the left of my right ear, blink wildly, like a trapped moth.

I crumble a cake. "Say on, Vizier." There is no use in prolonging his agony. Our agony.

"It came to the ears of the Third Priest of Amon late yesterday"—the Third Priest being another troublemaker, although less so than his predecessor Lord Rensonb, the news is bound to be bad—"that . . . that an unheard-of event has taken place."

Hapusoneb coughs, and his thin old chest wheezes. "In His Majesty's temple . . . in the holy-of-holies . . . in Amon's very sanctuary itself . . ."

My cool and calm and self-possessed Hapusoneb is so flustered that his eyes meet mine squarely. Realizing his blunder, he sinks to his knees in a state of abject confusion. I steel myself for an overwhelming disaster.

"Come, Vizier, complete your report." My voice is brisk. Pharaoh's duty is to maintain *maat*, the rightness of things, through all calamity.

Hapusoneb pulls himself together. "As His Majesty is aware, in the holy-of-holies of His Majesty's temple are niches, many of them. To use for the burning of candles. For the storage of ritual equipment, bowls for offerings, that sort of item. The recesses are covered by small folding doors. The doors, opening inward, hide the side walls of the niches."

I know all this as well as he does, but there is no way to hurry my Vizier. If he is ever called on to announce a flood or an enemy attack or an imminent earthquake, we will all be dead before he gets the words out.

"Last evening a priest went to remove a gold vessel from one of these niches. His hand caught somehow in the door and ripped it from its fastening. The wall behind it was exposed. On it was carved a small kneeling figure with the glyphs of the name—" Hapusoneb pauses, head bowed as if awaiting the executioner.

"The name?" But I know already.

"That of the Steward of Amon, Lord Senmut, Majesty."

There is a massive silence that can almost be seen, riveted in place by two shafts of sunlight from the high windows. Ah, Amon, thou tormentest thy daughter with another calamity. Thou seizest the rope of destiny from her hands and rendest it. . . .

"Have you confirmed this, Vizier?" Despite all effort my voice is faint.

"Majesty, this morning I went there. In each of the cupboards, and they are numerous, are painted figures or else statuettes of the Chief Steward. There are close to one hundred of them." The last words are whispered. The Vizier drops to his knees, more from weakness than respect.

Ah, Senmut, how couldst thou! I loved thee, I have told thee my secret thoughts, I have kept nothing from thee—and thou hast betrayed me!

But wait, it could be a conspiracy between the Third Priest and . . . not Hapusoneb, he is too honest in spite of his jealousy of My Friend . . . but someone who wishes to discredit Senmut. Yes, surely it is an evil trick. But still the words echo through my mind like drumbeats: "The lower a man's birth, the more help he needs to attain the Hereafter."

My whole body turns numb, as when one swallows a poisonous potion. Senmut could not commit such sacrilege. In my own temple possibly—and that would be bold beyond measure—but in the sanctuary of the God of Gods? The numbness stretches out to my mind. I cannot think. I wish not to think.

But think thou must, Hatshepsut, beloved daughter of Amon. An indignity has been enacted against thy holy father, and thy duty it is to punish the offender.

"But not my love, not Senmut," I whisper. Do not feel, Hatshepsut—*think*. Art thou a woman defending thy lover—or art thou Pharaoh, doing thy duty?

Hapusoneb's head is still fastened to the floor.

"Rise," I command. His bones creak as he unfolds his legs to stand, tottery and unsteady as a flimsy table. "Send the lord Senmut to me."

"At once, Your Majesty." He hobbles from the room, bent with misery.

I draw a long breath and ponder. *Is* Senmut capable of the act?

A memory comes to mind. Senmut once had ordered a statue of himself for his House of Eternity. The prayer inscribed on the statue read:

That Mut may give glory in heaven and on earth to the spirit of the Chief Steward of the King, Senmut; *that she may give the offerings which are in the Southland to the spirit of the* Magnate of the Tens of Upper and Lower Egypt, Senmut; *that she may give the food which is in the Northland to the spirit of the greatest of the great, the noblest of the nobles, the* Chief of the Mansion of the Red Crown, Senmut; *that she may give everything which comes forth from her offering-table in 'Most-Select-of-Places' and in (the temple, of the gods of Upper and Lower Egypt) to the spirit of the* Privy Councillor, Senmut; *that she may give evocations of bread and beer, beef and fowl and a drinking of water at the flood, to the* Chief Steward of Amon, Senmut, *who filled the storehouses and enriched the granaries, the* Overseer of the Double Granary of Amon, Senmut, *the justified, engendered of the worthy Ramose, the justified, and born of Hatnufer . . .*

The glory my Sole Companion took in those titles! Collecting and displaying them as a merchant exhibits his fondest wares. All my officials have hinted of his pride. I have been blind. This overweening pride has toppled his good sense.

My temper bursts its bonds, as a desperate prisoner rends his fetters. Where I have been numb, I now quiver with rage. To repay my goodness with mockery!

A figure bows itself into the chamber. Senmut. I wait until he stands before me, his face gentle, inquiring.

"Lord . . . thou . . . you exceed yourself!" My voice, harsh and strident, could belong to a street vendor.

His shoulders jerk with shock. For an instant his eyes gaze into mine.

"Highness . . . how?" He speaks in a murmur.

"Didst thou know? . . . Was it by thy . . . your . . . command? . . . The statues of yourself in the holy-of-holies of my temple?"

His face dissolves into guilt, into a question, reforms, wearing an expression of dignity. The dignity infuriates me further.

"Majesty, I meant no disrespect. The figures were hidden that none might know—none but the God of Gods, Amon, who through them would recognize the existence of your servant. Of *his* servant. For otherwise I am beneath his notice. He might then speak in my behalf to Osiris."

He speaks quietly, lucidly, without shame. Why is he not ashamed? Does he equate his rights with mine? No one does that to Pharaoh. Were a dagger, a sword,

within reach, I should slay him. My fury drives me mad.

"What presumption! None but Pharaoh travels the Underworld under Amon's protection. Even you as confidant of Pharaoh have not that privilege."

"Majesty, my intentions are sincere. . . ." His voice trembles as he tries to placate me.

"Leave me! You have betrayed my trust."

"Never that, Majesty! I would never betray thee. Only through love of thee were the statues placed in Amon's sanctuary."

His stricken face invites my pity. A part of me reaches toward him in tenderness . . . a part soon demolished by my rage.

"By now the priesthood—Amon's entire priesthood—knows what you have done. Knows of your audacity. If I accept the situation, it will say, 'How like a woman, to melt with forgiveness. Our pharaoh is no king, merely a softhearted queen!' What an impossible position you place me in!"

"I admit it." Senmut puts his hand on my shoulder.

I shake it off. The admission of the act helps me not at all.

"Hatshepsut, if thou wouldst say nothing . . . ignore the matter . . . in a few weeks' time the affair would be forgotten."

In my heart I know he is right. Senmut is always right. Perhaps it is that fact that most incenses me. Still, my temper rages in my heart like a wild beast.

"Go! Thou . . . You have disgraced the holy-of-holies. You have disgraced *me*."

"I go for now, Hatshepsut. But remember—my action was not sacrilege, it was love. For truly I love thee dearly and would never harm thee in any way."

I turn my back, and he bows his way out.

My frustration at Thutmose, at Egypt's restless neighbors, at the futile attempt on my life, at myself for growing old—all fuse together to form a spear aimed at Senmut.

I send for my Vizier, give curt orders that the statues be crushed to powder, the fine quartzite sarcophagus in the tomb under my temple, designed for Senmut, be smashed with the heaviest of hammers. Still furious, I stride up and down my chamber. Ingratitude, impertinence, irreverence—this is my reward for raising this . . . this *nobody* to the rank of Pharaoh's Favorite.

The servants tremble, drop dishes, stumble over themselves and one another in their panic, and desire to be unnoticed. My courageous Henut screws her bones into unaccustomed activity, brushes my hair herself, creams my face, rubs oils into my aching back, all without uttering one word.

Only, as she fetches me the goblet of wine I take at bedtime, she says in a wheedling tone, "Judge him gently, lady. A good friend he has been to you."

I give no answer, for the black mood is yet on me, the temper that I have never been able to bridle until it runs its course.

The next morning, after the Awakening of the

Morning ceremonies, I sense a new undercurrent of dread and anxiety. No more sad tidings, I trust. Pharaoh has his limits, too.

The Third Priest of Amon, with his touch of a swagger, hesitates just inside the door. The very one who informed on Senmut.

"Well?" I demand coldly.

"Majesty . . . a death. A . . ." His pretension falters under my look.

"Death? Who is dead?"

"The . . . lord Senmut, Majesty." There is a hint of smugness in the voice.

The room mists, screams with silence, finally clears. My hands grip the armrests of my throne like talons.

"It is not true! Lord Senmut was here yesterday. Why do you lie?"

The man's assurance dribbles from him till he is more terrified than my maids.

"Your Majesty, I myself did not see him. The news arrived this morning, minutes before the ritual. Pardon me for upsetting His Majesty. I thought . . . I expected . . ."

He had expected me to be pleased with his information. Gossip of my fiery audience with Senmut has spread throughout No-Amon. This palace holds secrets as securely as a sieve holds water.

I glare at the foolish little man in disbelief. Perspiration drips from his face onto the tile in big drops. But I am exhausted from yesterday's wrath—I can conjure up no more. Luckily for him. Once again the numbness seizes me; I cannot grasp the import of his news.

"How did this . . . this thing happen?"

"Last night ruffians, thieves, set on my lord in the evening's dark. He was stabbed."

"The assassins?"

"Dead also, Majesty. At my lord's cries the guards ran up and slew the men. Three of them. They were nobodies, low men. Surely they intended to rob him. Naturally an inquiry will be instituted."

"Why was not My Majesty informed at once?"

The pavement is discolored with his perspiration. He shakes as with an ague.

"There was felt no need. . . . I . . . No one wished to disturb His Majesty's rest. Since the lord died at once . . . and being in disgrace . . ."

"He was not in disgrace!" I hiss. "Hold your tongue, fool!"

My majestic serenity has disappeared. I conduct myself not like Pharaoh but like some irrational mortal. And I do not care.

"The guards . . . they should have taken the murderers alive."

"Exactly what I myself said, Majesty." He nods violently, scattering drops like a fountain.

"The guards are to be punished." I eye the Third Priest with half a mind to pack him off to prison or the torture.

He reads my thoughts and his eyes widen. "Immediately! Oh, immediately, gracious Majesty." Like a caterpillar, but more swiftly, he folds himself from the room.

With stately step I depart the chamber, gain my refuge, my own little room. There the terrible news reaches my heart. In silence I weep and writhe in grief. Beyond the simple bereavement is a piercing regret.

Why, oh why was I so harsh with my love? Imprudent and brash it was to install the statues. But brashness was part of his nature. Without it he would never have reached his position of Pharaoh's Favorite. I had encouraged that brashness—so long as it served me.

With bitter tears I mourn his loss. Hatshepsut, thou hast too few friends to risk losing one—and he the best one of thy life. I know, my heart, I know. For the remainder of my life I will repent that I upbraided him. With anguish I will blame myself for his death.

This is my punishment. I have violated *maat* and thus displeased my divine father, Amon, who orders that all be in accord with the natural harmony of the universe. Pharaoh is no exception. Pharaoh has been singled out as the target of Amon's wrath. Ah, I have paid for my transgressions for years to come!

Later, in a calmer mood, I ask myself, Why would anyone destroy Senmut? What has the murderer to gain?

The answer is not difficult. The crime was committed to isolate me, that I be left with no friend, no confidant, no defender. The rare moment was chosen when Senmut was in disfavor, so that I myself could be suspected of his death. Oh, Prince . . . thou and thy friends are as cunning as fiends!

He has worked slowly, my stepson. Slowly and carefully. He has set the priesthood against me, and the army. Now he cuts off my friends at court. Only my council is left me, a group of old, weary men, tired of governing and hopeful of retiring soon to their villas.

Some slight consolation I might have, could I have discovered the connection of Senmut's assassins with his enemies. Since these are dead, that solace is denied me. The guards are flogged to death as a reminder to others not to overdo their duty.

Senmut is buried in the cliff near his village home, close to the tomb of his parents. Nearby are buried the coffins of his little mare and his pet ape.

On a secret visit to his House of Eternity, I make a curious discovery. A fragment of a funerary relief that he had ordered years ago flakes away. Under a coat of plaster lies another set of reliefs. One explanation occurs to me: In fear lest his enemies, in an attempt to destroy his *ka*, might demolish the upper reliefs, Senmut had the others painted as a precaution. He was always a careful man.

I order that prayers be said, all manner of incantations from the Book of the Dead be placed in his tomb, amulets enclosed in his coffin, daily food offerings to be given for many years—in short, all done to ensure his safe passage to the fields of Ialu.

For what if I arrive at those fields to find no Senmut

to share eternity with me? My fault it would be for ordering the statues shattered. Fear not, dear Friend. I, daughter of my father Amon, and my own daughter, Nefrure, will guide thee safely home.

But for now . . . tomorrow I commence the project of opening the eastern mines. I alone. Take care, you priests of Amon. I have lost my Sole Companion, but *you* have lost a mediator. Henceforth my arrows against you will be no longer dulled but tipped with poison.

CHAPTER 19

Year 22 of the Reign
of His Majesty Makare Hatshepsut

I have done as I promised. After six years of being
worked, the mines produce well, discharging blocks
of gold, which mostly disappear into the cavernous
craw of Amon's priesthood. My father Amon it was
who placed me on the throne—and it is Amon who
demands an ever-mounting price for his favor.

The Prince, too, pays me back in my own currency.
Amon showed me his divine will in a dream (that of
declaring his daughter Hatshepsut ruler of Egypt). To
Thutmose he displayed a different will, in that fan-
tastic scene in the temple where his image appeared
to bow to my stepson. *I* recognized the spectacle as a
trick of the priests to defy me, but Thutmose, they tell
me, has ever regarded it as a sign of Amon's love for
him. He deludes himself.

For twenty-two years now I have reigned. Only

eight years remain until I celebrate my jubilee—my first jubilee, for I plan to have many. A jubilee is celebrated after thirty years, but one may cheat a little. Perhaps I will wait only two or three years before celebrating mine.

I am not old—I possess the vigor and strength of a youth. With Henut's potions of asses' milk and honey to remove wrinkles, and a plaster of powdered alum to firm my skin, I retain my beauty. However, I no longer chafe at being readied; if, with her brush and kohl, the girl can smooth a few years from my brow, I happily submit.

In an old scroll I came on a formula for restoring hair which I am tempted to put to use, despite the foulness of the ingredients.

Recipe for making the hair to grow, which was made for Tesh, mother of the Majesty of the Southern and Northern Kingdoms, Seti, deceased. Paws of a cat, one part; seeds of the grape, one part; hoof of a donkey, one part. Mix with oil, cook thoroughly in an earthern pot, and anoint herewith.

Henut's eyes lighted when she heard; the more loathsome the remedy, the more she approves.

Henut needs to apply some of her innumerable remedies to herself, to her personality as much as her person. She is as able as ever but inclined more and more to be grumpy and querulous. On the whole, her complaints cause me amusement rather than irritation.

Yesterday she came running to me full of injury. "The royal bodyguard is a pack of fools! They understand no word of our language. *Must* foreigners and barbarians be put to guard Thy Highness?" (Henut has taken to addressing me as "thou," as though she considers us of the same rank.)

"Why not? They guard me well. If they do not speak or understand our tongue, perhaps that is an advantage."

"I ordered one to move a chair and he merely stood, grinning like a monkey."

"That is not the work of a guard. A serving man will move what you wish."

I allow Henut, and only Henut, to bicker and chatter as she will, when no one else is about. Henut, that wizened, wrinkled, creaky creature, has become a kind of intimate friend. Few of those remain to me.

Nehesi is old and infirm and keeps to his bed. Hapusoneb made his journey westward last year, Ineni a year before that. My Second Priest of Amon, Puyemre, totters about his duties, reciting the liturgies with as much feeling as a parrot.

What Henut says is true. My guard and the army now consist largely of barbarians, mercenaries, and men conscripted by the provincial governors. Egyptians are too prosperous and well fed (I will take credit for that) to enter the army voluntarily. "Leave that to the foreigners," they say.

My country has never cheerfully supported an army. We lie too protected by our deserts to need defense, and we are too complacent to attack other lands— except as chastisement. To be honest, I have never favored a strong army. Contrarily, my father *did*, and my stepson *would*.

One was and one is a martial man, which leads to a disagreeable notion. Can it be that in other ways as well as this one the Prince is as able a man as his grandfather? It is impossible. The thought is repugnant, and I reject it.

Other thoughts of Thutmose I cannot reject, repugnant or not. Yesterday the Commander in Chief of the Army had audience with me. He is a dull man in all respects except the military, at which he is sharp indeed.

He comes right to the point. "Majesty, disturbing reports are received. A league of Syrian princes grows stronger each day. More and more provinces are persuaded to join."

"You believe they will attack Egypt, Commander?"

"No, Majesty. But they consider escaping Egypt's protectorate, to halt their tribute."

What a bother. Unable to lead troops, I have strengthened the Two Lands internally but not externally. Perceiving this, the vile Syrians become arrogant, and like clumsy lion cubs are ready to take on the world.

"My Majesty will send a letter of reproach and warning for their behavior."

Commander pulls a mournful face. "Possibly, Majesty . . ." He hesitates.

"Continue."

His words erupt in a frightened rush. "Possibly, after all, the Prince should be allowed to do . . . that which he wishes to do."

Thutmose again. Must he be thrown in my teeth by everyone?

"Clarify your statement, Commander."

"The Prince argues that he has made a Divine Contract with Great God Amon. In return for a lavish share of the booty of conquest—fields and property, monopolies, slaves, gold—the god will promote the imperialistic designs of the Prince. Naturally the priesthood benefits along with Amon. Unpleasant as the news is, Majesty, I fear it is genuine."

"Amon is My Majesty's protector, not the Prince's."

"Just so, just so. Unfortunately, the Prince believes he is chosen by the god to wage war against the eastern lands. Needless to say, the priesthood upholds him. Like the coalition of the Syrians, the body of Amon's priests grows immensely powerful."

Indeed, the Commander's news is disturbing. It is unbearable.

"Thank you, my Commander. I will give the matter my careful consideration."

But what is there to consider? I have little hold over my stepson. Despising one another, we avoid each other. From time to time I glimpse him racing his chariot over a desert road, from it shooting arrows at a target (his marksmanship cannot be faulted). They say his stamina is remarkable; he can march for days without food or rest.

Those activities I find myself envying. My one regret in life is that I was not born a man, with a man's physical strength and endurance (my mental prowess is topped by no man's). I could have conquered the world for the Two Lands. In doing so, I should have become the greatest of Egypt's great kings. It appears now that this is Thutmose's ambition. What gall to imagine that he might yet succeed. A presumptuous, ill-born upstart to subvert me!

Hatshepsut, thou corruptest thyself. For I believe that everyone—even Pharaoh—is born with a wild beast caged inside his heart. The degree to which he restrains that beast marks his level of *maat*, of civilization. I look into my heart and despair. For all my serene mask, inwardly I rage like a panther at my stepson, at the priesthood, for which I have done so much and which now thinks to betray me.

In times past a God-King made no bargains with priests, with anyone, being respected, adored, and feared for his godliness. Today the priesthood respects little, adores and fears not at all. It even presumes to dictate to Pharaoh. Early kings had their servants and attendants put to death and buried with them to serve them through eternity. Our beliefs have truly deteriorated.

Yet how much I must depend on the priests. Without them, when it comes my time to join my father the sun, how can I mingle with the gods without the help of the priesthood? Lacking their magic, how can I avoid in the Underworld the huge serpent Apophis, he who attempts to destroy the sun itself on its nightly voyage under the earth?

A son is responsible for his father's tomb, for the ceremonies in honor of his *ka*. There remains no one to do this for me, apart from a paid *sen* priest. Nefrure and Senmut are dead. I have no living issue—except for a stepson who would gladly effect my second death, efface my soul.

He has attempted my first death—he or his partisans. In ancient times the king wore an amulet, the *menyt*, hung in the back between his shoulders to afford protection, since the vulnerable place to strike is a person's back. Perhaps I should don such an amulet. . . .

One boon I am thankful for: My enemies are one fewer. Only a few months ago my old adversary Rensonb rested from life, the result of weak lungs rather than his weak stomach.

Hatshepsut, what ails thee? Thou wast never before a coward, wearing a shrunken, shriveled, fearful heart. Remember thy lifetime precept: resolution. Ah, but resolution has no effect on a failing destiny. Often now I sense that mine is on the wane. Like a falling star it rushes downward to its ruin. Because of the Prince?

Senmut was wont to drop hints. "Should the Prince suffer an accident while driving his chariot, if a lynchpin were to drop out, life would regain its serenity."

I considered his words. At best I disliked the Prince; at worse resented him, despised him. Never have I felt for him the hatred he bears me. Moreover, I share my father's feeling that the weak alone turn to murder to destroy the opposition. To me Thutmose was ever a challenge, a man on the *senet* board, to defeat by skill, not by brute force. I have never lacked skill.

Enough of dreary thoughts. This afternoon I have audience with my Overseer of the Royal Mines. It is to be hoped this conference is a happier one than that with my Commander in Chief. Overseer of the Mines Nekhti is a young man who has been in my service for two years. He reminds me somewhat of Senmut, with his quick mind, his unfailing good nature, his bold ideas. But only somewhat, for he has not the genius of my Sole Companion, not the charm, the warmth. Senmut was wholehearted in his affection, while in Nekhti, for all his courtesy, I sense a certain reserve.

Strangely, both Hapusoneb and Ineni opposed his appointment.

"What are your reasons?" I demanded.

"His character has not the straightness of *maat*, but curves, like His Majesty's golden crook," was Hapusoneb's answer.

Ineni pondered and mumbled and finally admitted, "There is no obvious reason, Majesty, a feeling, no more . . . the feeling one has in passing a desert copse where a panther crouches."

Well, both were growing old, both were unwell, their judgment was impaired. Lord Nekhti has served me well.

Today he comes to report on the gold mines in the Wady Hammamat, those which have produced gold sufficient to pave the streets of No-Amon.

"Your servant, Majesty." Nekhti kisses the floor before my throne.

"Rise, Lord Nekhti. The mines go well, I am sure."

He stands before me, eyes downcast, sporting a kilt of striped linen, blue, green, white. Colors in robes remind me always of the garish dress of the Syrians; nothing is more fresh than our pure white linen. But I am old-fashioned in this regard.

"I returned but yesterday from inspecting the great mine, O Majesty. It flourishes."

"The miners are content?"

Nekhti is surprised. "Content? The miners are convicts, Majesty, criminals, prisoners of war, those condemned for treason to the state. They are fettered, they work day and night. Their guards are foreigners who cannot communicate with them."

"My Majesty is aware of that. My meaning is, have they adequate food and clothing?"

He shakes his head. "The climate is too warm for clothing. As for food, they are provided water and bread. The bread is coarse but it is . . . bread."

"Conditions at the mines are said to be rigorous. One accepts this, seeing the prisoners merit such treatment. But if they lack sustenance, they will die. A dearth of workers will deprive Egypt of her gold."

Nekhti laughs a harsh little laugh. "There is no danger of that. We can invent crimes. We can capture a few Nubians across the border. We can commandeer slaves."

His callousness shocks me. Is the Black Land so heartless with her prisoners? This is a subject I should know more of.

"Describe to me, Overseer, the process of mining."

He bows, reflecting. "The rock in this area, Majesty, is black, while the veins bearing the gold ore are of a shining white quartz. The contrast is startling. An engineer chooses the most promising veins and sets the men, several thousand of them, to work with pick or chisel of copper to break up the quartz. Aboveground this is simple to do."

"In the shafts underground—how can the men see?"

"Each wears a candle fixed to his forehead. As they cleave the stone it falls in chunks to the floor of the mine, where it is gathered by young boys."

"Children are adjudged criminals, then?"

"No, Majesty. They are the offspring of wrongdoers. Often the families accompany the prisoners to the mines, and these, too, must work. The boys carry the fallen fragments to the surface. Here women and older men are employed to grind the pieces between two flat granite millstones until the quartz is reduced to mounds of white powder.

"For the final operation, the powder is carried to broad tables set at a slight inclination. Those in charge here are the most trustworthy of the prisoners. Their work is the least arduous in the mine, and they receive an extra ration of bread. Oh, they are well treated, Majesty," Nekhti assures me.

I recall Mother's cosmetics woman, Pekey, the one I disliked. She had been captured during my father's campaign in Nubia. Her family—parents, brothers, and sisters—possessing none of Pekey's skills (or wits either, perhaps), had, although royalty, been sent to the mines. I shuddered. Poor Pekey.

"Continue," I order Nekhti.

"The powder is spread on the tables and water poured over it. The people rub their hands over the powder, gently, so that the lighter matter flows off with the water, leaving the heavier particles. This process is repeated over and over till a good quantity of gold remains. This then is collected, mixed with lead, salt, tin, and barley, poured into pottery crucibles, and fired in a furnace for five days. When cooled, the crucibles are broken, revealing the ingots of pure gold."

"Your account is enlightening, Overseer. My Majesty thanks you." Moved by a sudden impulse, I ask, "Will you take a cup of wine with me, Lord Nekhti? Your tale gives me a thirst."

Gratified, he accepts. I send a servant for the wine. We converse of trifling affairs, of court gossip, at which he is glib, even clever in a malicious way.

All at once I feel weary and dull and bored. Why did I ever find this man charming? He is as brittle as an eggshell. We sip our wine, and I wait a polite moment to dismiss him.

"Majesty!" he exclaims. "I had forgotten. You may wish to see this."

Plucking something from a leather bag tied to his waist, he holds it out to me. It is a white stone, very rough, very shiny.

"Quartz, Majesty, from the mine." He points out the flecks of gold, traces a tiny vein running along one side. I examine it with interest.

"Keep it, Majesty. As a memento of the wealth of Egypt. May it increase a thousandfold." He laughs. A donkey's bray.

I thank him and bid him farewell. His conversation has depressed me. This has not been a good day; the stars strive against me. I think only sad, defeated thoughts.

Courage, Hatshepsut, and resolution. Dwell on the achievements of thy reign. According to Nekhti, the mines do well; the Two Lands remain wealthy and prosperous. I take credit for putting that wealth to proper use for the glorification of my country. I have added to the temple of Amon, erected two obelisks there, the tallest in the world. I have restored the temple of Hathor, my dear goddess, at Cusae, and other monuments up and down the Nile. Trading relations with Byblos, Libya, the southern lands, are again excellent, so that stacks of timber, piles of ivory tusks, logs of ebony, lie heaped on No-Amon's docks.

My expedition to Punt has been acclaimed an outstanding accomplishment. The copper and turquoise mines of the Sinai have been reopened. I have built for myself the most beautiful temple in Egypt and, in that desert valley where my father lies, an ornate tomb. In all the years of my rule I have corrected corruption and maintained peace. It is a record of which to be proud.

Above all, I have defied tradition to do what no woman has done before: crown herself king. That alone will set me with the stars. No one in a thousand years will equal *that* achievement!

In all these endeavors I have never forgotten for whom they were performed . . . for the people of the Two Lands. What good is a temple without people to worship in it? My obelisks stand to make Egyptians proud to be Egyptians. My father taught me that lesson.

Once when I was a child, our boat returned to No-Amon from an excursion upriver. Father ordered his and my chairs to be carried through the poor section of town, the streets so narrow I could reach out and touch the walls on either side. What impressed me were the odors: the sweat and ammonia, the cooking fires and garbage, the heavy scent of the adjoining bakery and brewery, all so overpowering I held my nose.

Father, noting me, exclaimed, "No, daughter! Remember always, this is *thy* country. The smells belong to that country. Smell deeply, deeply of them!"

I sigh for my memories and call for Henut. Perhaps with her soothing fingers she can massage away some of my sadness.

But no. Even Henut is as full of sighs as a palm tree.

"Eh, Highness. It seems thou must search out new mines."

Her words strike like arrows. "What do you mean?"

"The mine at Wady Hammamat is played out. So informed me the servant of Lord Nekhti. The booby gives himself airs. He prattles on all his master's acts."

"You did not hear well, woman, you grow deaf. The mine *does* produce well."

Henut's hands move from my head to her hips. She rears back in indignation.

"Lady, I hear like a hawk. The serving man himself observed the prisoners who lay or sat with no occupation. No more veins of the white rock can be found in that region."

I sit up. "Why would Nekhti weave me such a tale? He assured me the mine yields blocks of gold as readily as a man shapes bricks."

"He wishes to ease thy mind. A well-spoken man, that lord. But maybe not to be trusted, lady, being a good friend to the Prince." Henut grimaces her disdain of Thutmose.

I stare at her in amazement. "How do you know this? It cannot be true. My 'Eyes and Ears' has informed me of nothing of this."

Henut's face mirrors pride; she is for once more

knowledgeable than I. "The serving man told me only yesterday. He is a tattler. Like a net he leaks news of his master. He has served him less than a month, and most of that time he passed at the mine."

Why would Nekhti bespeak me these lies? Unless . . . by advising the priesthood and the army of the truth behind my back, he thinks to panic them into demands to send the Prince to war.

The matter is urgent. I must convene my council. I cannot. Not tonight. I am weary, weary. Tomorrow will be time enough.

"I will see to it, Henut, in the morning. Now brush my hair."

In my heart I know the affair should not wait an hour, a minute. The lies must be investigated at once. A curious apathy, like a cloud of incense, enfolds me. I, Hatshepsut the resolute, do nothing.

When the servants bring my dinner, I have no appetite but much malaise, no strength but a fevered head. This is no moment for illness. Tomorrow at dawn I must inform my Vizier of the conflicting stories of Nekhti. Something must be done about conditions at the mine. Treasurer can tell me how much gold. . . . In my mind the ingots of gold turn to lumps of stone which weigh down my head.

After I fall into my bed, exhausted beyond words, I am troubled with dreams—dark, deep, shadowy dreams of death. Death . . . a state I have prepared for all my life as we Egyptians do, propitiating the gods, building and furnishing our Houses of Eternity.

In my burial chamber is chiseled, *Hatshepsut living, living forever*, the words repeated over and over, which repetition makes truth of the statement. Also chiseled are the glyphs *Hatshepsut, beloved daughter of Amon.*

And yet . . . as a girl I said, "Henceforth I will do only what I, Hatshepsut, *wish to do.*" Have I in truth followed Amon's will . . . or have I artfully compelled Amon to follow *my* will? I jerk my mind from the disquieting question as I would my hand from the fire.

Resolution, Hatshepsut. Pharaoh shall have no fear, for Pharaoh travels in the company of the sun and stars. Nor shall I dread the Judgment. From the Book of the Dead I know the questions that will be asked, the answers to be given. I have the instructions for avoiding the traps and monsters of the Underworld.

By name I will address the assessor gods: Breaker of Bones, Eater of Blood, Swallower of Shades. I will deny to them a series of sins long as a line of soldier ants.

"I did not murder, I did not revile, I did not cause fear, I did not gossip, I did not show bad temper (well . . . but not often, not *very* often). I have not made any man work beyond his strength, I have not multiplied words in speaking, I have not committed any sin against any man (not against thee, my stepson, despite thy beliefs—the throne I took at Amon's bidding). I was not an eavesdropper, I was not proud (proud of my achievements, but there is no evil in that). There is no sin in my body. Let me go, ye gods. Ye know that I am without fault, without evil, without crime; I have lived on truth, I have been fed on truth. My mouth and my hands are pure."

All these responses I know by heart. Still, much can go wrong. What if, in the terror of facing the judges, I forget? What if the Prince, in his hatred, should persuade the *sen* priests to deny my *ka* the food offerings? He could chisel away the reliefs of food painted in my House of Eternity, scratch out my name on all temples, all memorials, all scrolls in my burial chamber . . . and my soul is destroyed forever. What power the living possess over the dead!

Suddenly in a flash of light a truth bursts on me. Hatshepsut, thou didst wish above all else in the world to be Pharaoh of Egypt. Thou art that. For twenty-two years thou hast been that. Thou, a woman, hast made thyself King of the Two Lands, a feat that no one else in the world will ever surpass.

But . . . everything in life has its price. This is the price of thy wish: that thou mayest lose eternity.

Then so be it. I have chosen my destiny. And I would not exchange my reign as King for any consideration. No, not for the fields of Ialu, or to live forever among the stars with Senmut and Nefrure, or even to ride each day with Amon across the heavens in his sun chariot.

With acceptance, my spirit sinks like a tired bird into a nest of peace. The heaviness of my soul is gone and resolution returns. My friends diminish; my enemies multiply, but they will not defeat me easily.

Ah, how thirsty I am. And dizzy. Some malady is

pending. Taking a lamp from a table, I pad into my study, search through the chest of scrolls for a certain poem, one that old Tutami used to read to us, it being a favorite of his. I can see why. The words are calming to the spirit. Yes, here it is. By the snaking glow of the lamp I read:

I say to myself every day:
As is the convalescence of a sick person
Who goes to the Court after his affliction,
Such is death.

I say to myself every day:
As is the inhaling of the scent of a perfume,
As a seat under the protection of an outstretched
    curtain,
Such is death.

I say to myself every day:
As the inhaling of the odor of a garden of flowers,
As a seat upon the bank of the Land of
    Intoxication,
Such is death.

I say to myself every day:
As the clearing again of the sky,
As a man who goes out to catch birds with a net
And finds himself suddenly in an unknown land,
Such is death!

After finishing the poem, Tutami would add wryly, "It is particularly inspiring to read of death when one's life stretches as long as the Nile in front of one."

And so life stretches before me in spite of these curious fancies. I sink back on my couch. Hatshepsut, it is time thou didst develop a sense of humor. Until now thou hast cared so intensely about everything. What thou hast desired, thou hast desired with all thy heart and strength, against all odds . . . and there was no time for humor. But now . . .

All at once a gigantic wave of nausea passes over me. I bend over to ease the pain, and a scene of childhood passes before me. Henut scolds, "Sit up straight, young mistress. A princess must always have a straight back."

Oh yes, even more a queen, a king, must have a straight back. But my body will not obey my mind.

I am covered with perspiration, the room whirls about me. I must call Henut and the physician. My legs will not support me, my heart thumps loud as a war drum. What strange ailment has struck me?

"Henut! Someone! Come!" The call issues forth in a whisper.

Where are the guards? The palace is lifeless, silent as a tomb.

Poison. Someone has fed me poison. Who?

Of course. Nekhti. In my wine. He tricked me. A traitor, friend to Thutmose, placed in my service for this very purpose.

So, my stepson, in the end thou hast vanquished

me. Thou art the victor. *But only after twenty-two years.*

I cannot breathe; my hands are cold, so cold.

There is a crash. Oh, I have fallen, and a table with me.

Suddenly there is running, then lamps, then people . . . or are they only shadows? No, one is Henut, and she kneels, winds her arms about me. But I cannot feel them or her tears. Why does she weep? I am the Princess Hatshepsut, with the world before me.

Ah no, I am—I was—Great God Pharaoh of Egypt, His Majesty, Queen Hatshepsut. And the world is behind me.

EPILOGUE

As Hatshepsut had feared, Thutmose III, who immediately ascended the throne and ruled Egypt for the following thirty-five years, took full revenge on his stepmother. He smashed her sarcophagus, threw down her statues, hacked her name from countless memorials and temples up and down the Nile, sheathed her obelisks in plaster, possibly burned her mummy. He also released his wrath on the tombs of Senmut, Hapusoneb, Thuty, and other Hatshepsut officials, erasing their names from inscriptions.

Aside from these vengeful acts, Thutmose appears to have been a wise, humane, and energetic pharaoh. Syria, taking advantage of a female ruler, had begun during Hatshepsut's last years to rebel against Egypt's domination. On his accession to the throne, Thutmose and his army marched on the revolting princes and quickly quelled them. In the next twenty years this energetic king, bent on imperialistic conquest, was to extend Egypt's dominion to the farthest boundaries in its history. His building program rivaled that of Hatshepsut.

Little wonder, then, that Thutmose was described as "a lord of wings, who swoops down upon that which he sees" or "a circling comet that shoots out its flames and in fire gives forth its substance." Even taking into account the exaggeration of the Egyptians, Thutmose must be acknowledged as one of Egypt's greatest pharaohs.

And so, too, must Makare Hatshepsut, who also possessed the distinction of being a woman. Today her temple, the *zesru zeser*, is generally considered the most beautiful example of architecture practiced by the ancient Egyptians. Her two obelisks still stand at Karnak. The highly successful expedition to Punt was a major achievement of her reign.

But what the modern world finds most intriguing in Hatshepsut is the strong personality that braved a vigorous stepson and a powerful priesthood to declare herself King of Upper and Lower Egypt, and to rule as such for over twenty years.

PRINCIPAL CHARACTERS
AND GODS

Ahmose—*mother of Hatshepsut*

Amenmose—*brother of Hatshepsut*

Amon—*god of the sun, chief god of No-Amon*

"Eyes and Ears"—*Hatshepsut's Chief of Royal Security*

Hapusoneb—*Hatshepsut's Vizier, First Prophet of Amon, and member of her Council of Government*

Hathor—*goddess of love and beauty*

Henut—*Hatshepsut's childhood nurse and later her maid*

Ineni—*royal architect and member of the governing council during the reigns of Thutmose I, Thutmose II, and Hatshepsut*

Isis—*concubine in Thutmose II's harem and mother of Thutmose III*

Nefrure—*daughter of Hatshepsut and Thutmose II*

Nehesi—*Chief Treasurer and leader of the expedition to Punt*

Nekhti—*Overseer of the Royal Mines*

Osiris—*god of the Underworld*

Pekey—*Queen Ahmose's cosmetics maid*

Puyemre—*Second Priest of Amon and member of the council*

Rensonb—*Third Priest of Amon and a partisan of Thutmose III*

Senmut—*Hatshepsut's favorite courtier and chief adviser; also the architect of the* zesru zeser

Set—*god of the desert, often considered a god of evil*

Thutmose I—*Pharaoh and father of Hatshepsut*

Thutmose II—*Pharaoh and husband of Hatshepsut*

Thutmose III—*son of Thutmose II and Isis; stepson of Hatshepsut*

Thuty—*Hatshepsut's Chancellor and member of her council*

Tutami—*tutor of Hatshepsut and her brothers*

Wadjmose—*brother of Hatshepsut*

AFTERWORD

Some years ago, as I was leafing through Volume I of Will Durant's *Story of Civilization*, the chapter on Egypt caught my attention. After reading it more thoroughly, I found myself excited and intrigued by a long-dead civilization.

The humane and tolerant outlook of a people living in a time of general ruthlessness and cruelty was appealing. The more I read, both of ancient Egypt's history and of its customs, the more fascinated I became. That fascination peaked with the few facts known of Hatshepsut—a queen who, pushing aside her stepson, made herself pharaoh at a period when queen rulers were seldom tolerated.

In writing Hatshepsut's story, I took as framework the known facts and then molded around them the figure of the queen as I believe she was. Most of the other main characters in my story really existed, among them the Thutmoses, Senmut, Nefrure, although some minor characters were imagined. To embellish the story and make it more authentic I described those manners and customs of the ancient Egyptians which particularly interested me. Two books on which I relied heavily were Leonard Cottrell's *Lady of the Two Lands* and John Ewbank Manchip White's *Everyday Life in Ancient Egypt*. Where possible, I have drawn inspiration from the translations of Egyptian hieroglyphics by James Breasted, Sir Alan Gardiner, Pierre Montet, and W. Flinders Petrie.

Weaving together the facts, speculation, characters, and customs of that time became a game, rather like assembling a jigsaw puzzle. It was no less exact. I hope the readers of *His Majesty, Queen Hatshepsut* will enjoy the result.

89-10451

DATE DUE			
6B-2			
MAY 15 1990			
6-10			
OCT. 17 1990			